DEEP THOUGHTS FROM A

HOLLYWOOD
BLONDE

DEEP THOUGHTS FROM A
HOLLYWOOD BLONDE

JENNIE GARTH

WITH EMILY HECKMAN

 NEW AMERICAN LIBRARY

New American Library
Published by the Penguin Group
Penguin Group (USA) LLC, 375 Hudson Street,
New York, New York 10014

USA | Canada | UK | Ireland | Australia | New Zealand | India | South Africa | China
penguin.com
A Penguin Random House Company

First published by Signet, an imprint of New American Library,
a division of Penguin Group (USA) LLC

First Printing, March 2014

 REGISTERED TRADEMARK—MARCA REGISTRADA

LIBRARY OF CONGRESS CATALOGING-IN-PUBLICATION DATA:
Garth, Jennie, 1972–
Deep Thoughts from a Hollywood Blonde/Jennie Garth with Emily Heckman.
p. cm.
ISBN 978-0-451-24027-9 (hardback)
1. Garth, Jennie, 1972– 2. Actresses—United States—Biography.
I. Heckman, Emily. II. Title.
PN2287.G395A3 2014
791.4302'8092—dc23   2013044213
[B]

Printed in the United States of America
10 9 8 7 6 5 4 3 2

Set in Adobe Garamond
Designed by Spring Hoteling

To my three little birdies.
I love watching you fly.

"Setting an example is not the main means of influencing others, it's the only means."

—Albert Einstein

CONTENTS

CONTENTS

CONTENTS

DEEP THOUGHTS FROM A
HOLLYWOOD BLONDE

INTRODUCTION

Being a blonde is both a blessing and a curse. There's an assumption that if you're blonde you have no brains, and because you have no brains you're the life of the party, and when you're the life of the party, everything is easy and your life is carefree and . . . Wait a minute. Really? Is that what the world thinks of us?

My blondeness has long been one of my most identifying features, and at some point, it became part of my identity. So when I thought about what I wanted to call my memoir, I knew I'd have to capture the truth behind being a blonde. And it came to me: *Deep Thoughts from a Hollywood Blonde.*

I felt like this might be a good opportunity to debunk some myths about the fairest among us and, in my own personal case, demonstrate that some of the clichés about blondes are clichés precisely because they are so damn true. Surely I am the right person to write this book, because I am the rarest of blondes: a natural one.

1

Cliché number one: Blondes are dumb. Of course! People say this so often that it must be true! And let's not forget its ugly stepsisters: blondes are ditzy, naive, and have bad memories. In my case, the memory part is absolutely true: I happen to have the worst memory of any human being I have ever encountered.

My memory is so bad that the people closest to me actually feel comfortable joking about it, because they know I won't remember that they were just making fun of me. Recently I even had a series of CAT scans done of my brain, and I was certain that these detailed photographs would finally reveal the giant, gaping hole where my memory is supposed to be. Imagine my surprise—and horror—when the images revealed nothing more than a normal, run-of-the-mill brain. There was no weird eraser-shaped growth in there, no evidence of shrinkage or damage—there was nothing to explain why I can't remember so many things, including what I had for dinner last night.

You would think that having such a dim memory would make writing a memoir very, very difficult, but actually, once I got started, writing seemed to activate the dormant recollection part of my brain, and my life as I had forgotten it began to come back to me. The more I wrote, the more I remembered. And the more I remembered, the more I began to realize how good this process was for me. About halfway through, something even clicked, and I realized that by writing about my life, warts and all, I was really getting to know myself in a way that was at times humbling, at times horrifying, and definitely always eye-opening and entertaining.

On top of that, I know that there is an "e" at the end of the word *blonde*, so clearly I'm no dummy. So myth one—debunked!

Cliché number two: Blondes are bad drivers. In my case, totally false. One of the things I'm most proud of is the fact that I can parallel-park a forty-foot RV on La Cienega Boulevard in one shot. At rush hour. I've done this while watching many a guy struggle to maneuver a

Prius into a parking spot in a completely empty lot. I've also driven that very same RV across the country with four kids, two dogs, and a baby pig on board. Need I say more? Cliché number two, squashed.

Cliché number three: Blondes get more attention. True! But whether or not this kind of attention is welcome is another thing. I know every woman, regardless of hair color, has been on the receiving end of unwanted catcalls while she's minding her own business, or lame come-ons when she's out with friends. But for blondes, this kind of "attention" can be relentless. Let me tell you, it's a drag. And it doesn't help when you're a blonde who has been on several hit television shows and you are recognized wherever you go. ("There goes that blonde!") On the other hand, when you're a blonde, people assume you're the life of the party and so you're never left out. The downside of this is that you can never be the wallflower, not even when you might want to be.

Another blonde cliché: Blondes have more fun. This is a pretty complicated concept, believe it or not, because sometimes it's true; sometimes it's not. You'll have to read on to find out what blonde fun is all about!

In the end, I realized that by writing a book, I could, in my own humble way, represent for the fair-haired team, and show the world that we blondes actually do have something to say, at least when we can remember what it is.

And as it turns out, I have quite a lot to say.

I'm at a point where it's time to reflect. I went through a very public divorce, I am now on my own with my three kids, and I just crossed that tricky invisible line into my forties. Maybe because of all these things, or maybe despite them, in many important ways I feel like my life is just beginning. Could it be that there's something to share about starting over, or starting wiser, or just deciding that sometimes there's a story to be told in the middle of it all? And maybe it's a story that other people might *relate* to?

Opening myself up doesn't come naturally. I was in the media spotlight very young with the success of *Beverly Hills, 90210*, but I did my best to maintain my privacy and stay out of the tabloids. Until recently, of course, when my very public divorce thrust me into the spotlight. And yet I have never really shared my experiences or my side of the story. Very little is known about me or how I've gotten to this really gnarly, enlightening, important moment in my life.

I had to work up the courage to put my story down on the page. This meant owning up to all of the choices, mistakes, triumphs, and experiences that have propelled my life along in seemingly mysterious, often amazing, sometimes devastatingly painful ways. But once I got started, I realized that there is a great gift in this kind of stocktaking, because when I added up all these things, they became the story of me. And learning the story of me has been the most liberating experience of my life.

Writing this book has been the most challenging project I've ever taken on, and also the most illuminating and humbling. Revealing myself has never been my way. I mean, I've spent my life playing other people. But in writing this book, I've come to realize that in sharing ourselves, we become ourselves. My struggles are not unique, but my story is, and it's my hope that if I can share a little bit about myself, it will encourage you to do the same.

So thank you. From the bottom of my heart. For wanting to know me. For caring enough to buy this book. Thank you for the love. It means the world to me.

That's a Hollywood blonde for you. And these are her deep thoughts.
With gratitude,
Jennie

DOWN ON THE FARM

I come from very humble, very loving, very "normal people" stock.

My parents, John and Carolyn, who were both educators, met and married in small-town Illinois, where I was born and raised. Both my mother and father were married and divorced before they met, and each brought three kids from those first marriages to their union. This meant that, before they had me, they were a kind of real-life Brady Bunch. Which just so happened to be my favorite show while growing up.

Six kids. That is a handful for anyone, but John and Carolyn cemented their new union by having one child together, and that would be me: the runt, the miracle, the baby of this big, blended family, the blessed little link that joined the DNA of both sides of the Garth family. I am the youngest child by a full five years, and so I was, as you would expect, spoiled rotten. And not just by my parents, but by my four older sisters and two older brothers, and pretty much everyone else around me.

I was born in the bustling metropolis of Urbana, Illinois, a city of about forty thousand souls. When I was still just a baby, my parents moved me, my two brothers and sister on my dad's side, and my three sisters on my mom's side—whom my dad, John, legally adopted, so all seven of us siblings, in the end, are Garths—to a teeny, tiny spot on the Illinois map, a farming town called Arcola. There they bought a twenty-five-acre parcel of land outside of town and plunked us down in my dad's pink RV while they built us a house and farm, and I lived here with my mom and dad and my three sisters from my mother's first marriage.

Arcola, population roughly three thousand, is the home of Raggedy Ann and Andy, is the broom corn capital of the world, and, most glamorously, is the home of the Lawn Rangers, an award-winning precision lawn mower drill team. It's a sweet, sweet place that is smack in the middle of nowhere and so is utterly devoid of stress. At least, that's how I remember it.

From the time I was born, I shared a room with my sister Cammie, who is nine years older than me. I became her little doll, and she fawned over me and took me with her everywhere, and between Cammie and the rest of my family, my feet pretty much never touched the ground, which was a good thing, because I hated—still do—to get dirty.

My dad, an adult-education pioneer by day, was a rancher and farmer at heart, so he raised Tennessee walking horses and hay on our farm. All of us kids were supposed to do our fair share of chores, but one time, when I was asked to clean out the horse stalls, I burst into tears, and my blubbering was so devastatingly effective that I was never asked to do that chore again. The price for being excused from having to shovel shit was that I was given the nickname Puddles, which I was okay with. In fact, I learned to turn on the waterworks whenever I was called upon to do anything unpleasant. This could have been the origin of my interest in acting. Very quickly, I learned to smile or mug in just the right ways, so that no one in my family would stop adoring my lazy little self, and for the most part, this strategy worked.

I also, apparently, balked at ranch fashion early on and always wanted to wear dresses, the pinker and frillier the better. I was a girlie-girl from the get-go, and I got a lot of grief about this from my tougher, more outdoorsy older siblings, who wore work boots and overalls and hand-me-down T-shirts.

We lived on the county-line road, which didn't mean much to me; it was just like every other single-lane, barely asphalt road that stretched out endlessly through the corn and soybean fields. In the hot summer months, the black tar would heat up and loosen the gravel that would fling everywhere, like a million tiny firecrackers going off as we'd barrel down the roads in my dad's old blue Ford. I was always silently nervous that we were going to drift off into one of the ditches that outlined the tiny pathway on both sides, because of the big hump that ran right down the middle of that road. I could never understand what the big hump was for: Were they trying to make it a challenge to stay on the road? I'd hold my breath if ever another truck would come up on us and fly by at what seemed like a million miles an hour. There were grasshoppers everywhere and crickets singing what seemed like all day. The smell of fresh-cut grass is something that always makes me feel young again. During the summers my sisters and I would earn extra money "walking beans" for the neighboring farmers, which meant we'd go up and down the hundreds of perfectly planted rows of soybeans, pulling out any stray weeds. I, for some reason, loved this summertime job and the spare change it gave me. Something about cleaning the fields until they were absolutely perfect, as they were intended, never leaving the smallest rogue thistle behind, was deeply satisfying to me. We'd finish our days exhausted and sunburned, but I'd waste no time in begging my sister Lisa to fire up her Honda motorcycle and ride alongside me on my bicycle to the little antiques store about thirty minutes away, which also had a candy counter and a soda machine. We'd have to do this while my mom was at work, because she didn't like us eating sugar, so we'd sneak it big-time! And yes, I'd ride an hour straight just to sink my teeth into a Baby Ruth.

My neighbor at the end of the driveway was a little boy my age, Jeff. We became fast buddies, spending entire days together riding our bikes or playing his bitchin' Atari game. We would hide out in his bedroom with the bright blue shag carpet, joysticks in hand, and battle at Pong until his mom kicked me out at dinnertime, unless we were under the bridge pretending to be hobos, skipping rocks, keeping cool in the wet shade. Jeff was like my little brother; we were two little towheads, completely innocent and free.

I had a pony named Chocolate, and I loved him more than anything. I started riding when I was just two or three, and Chocolate, it is fair to say, became my best friend and closest confidant. I spent hours and hours with him, telling him my deepest secrets, getting to know every inch of our land. Chocolate was an incredibly patient, forgiving soul. My sister Wendy and I used to torment him by riding him at the same time, with me facing forward and Wendy facing his butt; then I'd try to make him run straight out, while Wendy would pull his tail hairs one at a time, trying to get him to buck and kick so that he'd give us a really wild ride. PETA, an organization that I love and have been a spokesperson for, is, I'm sure, calling someone as I type this. I was a country girl, for sure, but I was no American Girl doll; I could be mischievous and naughty. And I still can be.

When I wasn't with Jeff or Chocolate, I was out on my pink Huffy dirt bike, with its awesome white vinyl banana seat and wide-set handlebars. I'd ride that thing all over those twenty-five acres all by myself, totally unaware of how much freedom I had, which was an incredible amount. But all that time on my own made me feel safe and secure being outdoors, and I really grew to feel as though the farm itself had become a good friend to me, too. That piece of land was reliable and solid, and I was grateful for it. I'd cruise around and hunt for leftover corncobs, and then I'd gather them up and make little tepees with them in the barren cornfields. Or I'd pick wildflowers, or make my way down the thinly graveled road that led to the small cemetery that was situated on our property. Once I got there, I'd toss my bike down and step over the low chain-link fence that surrounded this tiny, still manicured plot of land, and I'd walk those rutted little paths between the broken, crooked headstones, and I'd talk to myself and read the names on the tombs and . . .

Wait a minute. Hold. The. Phone! Why, in the name of Michael Jackson, did my mom and dad buy a farm in the middle of nowhere, Illinois, with a cemetery on the property? Mind you, they didn't just do this once—they did it twice! Twice! Because this was the second property we'd lived on that had a cemetery on it. When I think about this now, I can't help but wonder what on earth my parents thought when they did this. Were they into some crazy pagan voodoo thing that meant they could buy only property that had a cemetery on it? Were they just sharing a morbid joke and planning ahead? Okay, I'm starting to get weird and obsessive about this, but really: What was up with those little graveyards? I mean, could it get any more *American Gothic*? Whatever the reason, the truth is that I find it much weirder to think about this than it actually was to live with them, because I found those private little sacred plots to be a great place to rest and collect my thoughts. Kinda weird, right?

When I look back, my childhood seems a bit lonely, and in some ways it was. But in other ways it wasn't at all. There were long days when my sisters were at school and I was on my own, hunting down woolly black caterpillars or lying on my stomach on those soft green mounds of earth in the graveyard. When I think back on this, I feel calm, because being around all those old bones and spirits didn't freak me out;

they kind of filled me with a sense of solace, maybe because I'm a bit of an old soul myself.

I spent a lot of time when I was young not talking to anyone, and so I ended up, both by nature and nurture, pretty shy and introverted. I'd like to think my shyness is more a function of always being alone rather than not wanting to be near other people, because I loved being around my family. I mean I *loved* it, and I couldn't get enough of it. And when they were off at work or school, I ended up spending a lot of my time alone and in my own head.

It was just me, a pale little girl with long white braids and all that space, all that sky. It was very *Little House on the Prairie*, for sure. It's where I developed my deep love of the land, my deep passion for animals (aside from the horses, we had dogs and cats and rabbits and . . .). It was where I learned to just love, love, love being outdoors. It's also where I did my first modeling job, when I was around seven. There I was, in my overalls and braids, and I was supposed to stand and smile in front of a cornfield, for a picture that would be featured in a brochure for the Corn Growers Association. Well, my nerves must have gotten the best of me, or else I ate too many bowls of Rice Krispies that morning, because on our way out to the photo shoot, I barfed all over the backseat of my mom's car and down the front of my shirt. My mom took my shirt off, wiped my hair, the ends of my braids, and the front of my overalls with it, and then—*snap!*—the picture was taken with me standing there in my overalls, my pigtails looking like bunches of young corn silk, the satisfied look of a kid who'd just barfed still on my face.

I wasn't adored just by all of my older siblings; I was also the undisputed apple of my dad's eye. My mom tells me that when I was a baby, my dad would come in from work in the late afternoon, scoop me up, settle down on the couch with me on his chest, and we'd both crash hard, me rising and falling on his big, burly chest, cozy and asleep. It was my favorite spot, a place I long for still to this day.

I idolized my dad from a very young age: He was the hero of our family, a man's man who loved his house full of girls with all his heart. He wasn't a talkative person (I definitely share this trait of his), but he was a solid person, a dependable person. I always knew I could count on him. And I stuck by him like a burr on a sock. We were so close, in fact, or so goes the family lore, that I decided to be born on his birthday. And I was, he liked to tell me, absolutely the best birthday present he ever got. To say we were close would be an understatement: I was the poster child for "Daddy's little girl."

"You were a pain in the ass," my sister Cammie laughingly said to me recently when I asked her what I was like as a kid. "You were into everything. Everything. And, man, you were just so damn cute." Ah, Cammie. I was also the apple of her eye, no doubt about it. Despite being almost a decade older than me, Cammie never gave me the brush-off, never made me feel like I was really in the way. Since we shared a room, she would get me ready for school and braid my hair in the mornings. I remember that I was in second grade when Cammie got her driver's license, and she'd drive me to school in her bitchin' El Camino, the radio blasting so loud that I'd burst into tears. That was my Cammie: driving good ol' Puddles to elementary school on her way to high school in her badass car.

I loved Cammie just as fiercely she loved me. I love all my siblings, every single one of them, but me and Cammie? We were thick as thieves. Two peas in a pod. All of those things and then some. All of my other siblings would do anything in the world for me, too. They are all just that kind of people: true-blue, kind, straightforward. Completely unpretentious. They are the salt of the earth, the Garths, and I'm proud to be one of them.

My mom, to this day, from time to time likes to tell me that her kids and John's kids would fight over whose family I most favored, whose sibling I really was. I was treated like a princess by everyone, like the little royal who united two households, joining them in everlasting love and harmony. I would be lying if I didn't say this went to my head, at least a little.

I'm sure I'll remember more about my life on that sweet farm, but until I do, I just want to say that our rural, very private, big and close family upbringing in Illinois was a truly beautiful thing. It was a solid start that I'm forever grateful for. But like most of the best things in life, it didn't last. It all got shaken up when my dad had a massive heart attack when I was nine. After that, things for the Garths were just never the same.

THE FIRST BIG BLOW

When I was a little girl, my dad had his first heart attack. It was a massive one. It was so bad it very nearly took my father out of the game, and his heart was so damaged by this episode that he had to undergo major open-heart surgery. Back then, this kind of surgery was pretty new and dangerous and super-risky. But my dad's heart was so badly damaged that there were just no other options: My mother was told that he had to have the surgery or he would surely die.

Fortunately for me, for all of us, my dad survived this awful ordeal, but he was never the same afterward. The blow to his heart pretty much knocked the stuffing out of him, and he emerged from the long rehabilitation that followed his surgery a different man—at least physically. He was no longer the invincible he-man of my child's mind, the burly guy with the chafed farmer's hands who could lift and bale and ride and wrestle. My dad came back rattled and tentative and visibly weakened. He had had a serious brush with mortality and this stuck with him, making him even more withdrawn and quiet than he had been before.

From then on, I always felt like I was waiting for some kind of terrible, terrifying shoe to drop. I was afraid that my dad was going to get sick again, or worse, he'd have another heart attack, and this time we wouldn't be so lucky and we would lose him. It was a horrible feeling that I just couldn't shake. I don't know if any of us could.

I was too young to understand it back then, but my dad had been diagnosed with heart disease at his young age, in his late thirties, specifically arteriosclerosis (hardening of the arteries). This was the same kind of heart disease that had killed his own father at a pretty young age.

Winters in Illinois are long and cold, and when your home is a working farm, you have to spend most of your days out of doors tending to the animals. Though my dad regained a lot of his strength after that brutal first heart attack, he was never a hundred percent again, and we all felt this overwhelming need to protect him, to figure out what we could do to keep him from putting any undue stress on his beleaguered heart. Caring for the farm in the middle of nowhere, especially during those pretty brutal Midwestern winter months, was no longer in my dad's best interest. All of us believed this.

So when I was twelve, we left our Illinois farm and headed for Phoenix, Arizona, where we had some distant family ties, and where, the doctors told him, the warm, dry weather would help heal him.

I'll never forget that move, which just felt so surreal, so strange; we were like a circus family, packing up all of our belongings, including our animals, all of our farming equipment—everything. We didn't have a lot of extra money, so we couldn't afford to hire a moving company to help us. I remember a caravan of our vehicles being lined up by the barn and then packed to the gills with everything we owned. We were making a family move, but only part of my family—my older sisters Wendy and Lisa—was coming with us. My older brothers and another older sister, and my Cammie—my protector, my big sister, my second mom—were not. Cammie was twenty-one and already married and settling into her own new family life, but this didn't make parting any easier for either of us. In fact, I would say it was pretty damn traumatic, leaving her like that.

I actually need to stop and think for a minute about the impact of this on both of us. I had been her baby even more than I'd been my parents', in many ways. She'd scoop me up and snuggle me into her life. I was like her real-life Polly Pocket doll: She took me everywhere with her, did everything with and for me from the moment I was born until the moment we pulled away from our farm. And . . . what on earth would I do without her by my side? How would I manage without her? I imagined it would be like having a bike without wheels. I don't think I've ever been able to really wrap my head around what a huge piece of my heart stayed with Cammie back in Illinois when we moved south to Arizona. But I can say that it was, at that point, absolutely the biggest loss I'd ever sustained, and one that I never quite got over.

But we Garths were on a mission, and that mission was to keep my dad alive. Whether we were staying back in Illinois or heading out to Arizona, everyone in my family was determined to be doing whatever had to be done to make sure our dad stayed around as long as possible. And if that meant my parents would sell their farm and move to Arizona, well, then that was what would happen. For me, as a girl just on the verge of adolescence, this didn't seem like a sacrifice; it just seemed like the right thing to do. And, of course, it was.

So we loaded up my dad's beat-up pickup truck and our ragtag bunch of old cars and off we went, tentatively hopeful about what the future would bring. I left the farm and all that quiet and space, and landed, with a loud thunk, in the giant, crowded megalopolis of Phoenix. I had never been in a city before; heck, I had never even set foot in a suburb. I was scared to death about going to a new school on my own. Of course, as the new girl, I was promptly teased and bullied, and I realized pretty quickly that I needed to pretend I was okay and keep a stiff upper lip, because Puddles just wasn't going to have a fighting chance here. So I sucked it up and forced myself to come out of my shell, and I threw myself into some activities so I wouldn't just crumple with grief and run off crying. I was such a fish out of water, such an outsider, that I did my ever-loving best to fit in. I became a cheerleader, and I took dance classes, and I wore the kinds of clothes the other girls wore, and I even did a bit of preteen modeling. Who knew that all of these slightly random, very lost-girl decisions would end up determining the trajectory of my life in such dramatic, almost made-for-TV-movie ways? Because, as it turned out, Arizona was just an uncomfortable, temporary landing pad for me. It was never home, not in any real, meaningful way; it was just a pit stop for a lonely young girl.

BIG BANGS AND UGLY BAND COSTUMES

Leaving Illinois was pretty traumatic, to say the least. I remember my mom throwing a good-bye barbecue at our remote twenty-five-acre ranch and I got to invite all of my friends—I think there were four of us, including me. On that, my last day in Illinois, my friends and I climbed trees and ate cake, and then said awkward good-byes. And that was it.

Next thing I knew, auctioneers were selling off most of our belongings, whatever didn't fit into the haggard assortment of cars and trucks and U-Hauls my parents had stuffed full of our stuff. (I remember them throwing the last odds and ends—blankets and such—into a horse trailer that was hooked up to my dad's pickup.) It would become the Garth family parade, pulled together by my parents and waved away by pretty much everyone I'd ever known in my life.

I never saw any of those childhood friends again. To this day, this fact just strikes me as very weird, and ever since then, I've never been a fan of moving on and not looking back. In fact, I've grown up to be the opposite of the kind of person who can just cut and run: I am loyal, loyal, loyal. So loyal that I am now intensely selective about the people I let in. I just cannot bear to let the people I love go. Once I bring someone in close, that's pretty much it. I am theirs.

The only people we didn't leave behind were just a few members of our immediate family. The others, as mentioned, had to stay back in Illinois: There was my sister Lynn and her family, my brother Johnny and his family, and my brother Chuck. And, of course, there was Cammie.

I have in my mind the horrible, awful memory of her sobbing and running after the moving truck I was seat-belted into, my tiny white poodle held firmly on my lap. I can still see her in the rearview mirror of my mind. It is an image that still haunts me and seems to offer a pretty succinct snapshot of what I think of as the PTSD (self-diagnosed, of course) that has contributed to my memory being as scattershot as it is a lot of the time.

Looking back, I guess that in some pretty real ways, that move marked the end of my storybook childhood. Because everything changed from then on out. My sisters Lisa and Wendy made the move to Arizona with us, but they were already doing their own thing by then: Lisa was going into college, I think, and Wendy had only a year of high school left, so Lord knew where she'd be heading off to soon.

Illinois is picture-postcard-pretty farm country: lush and green in the warm months, barren and cold in the winter months. It is one of those states with four classic seasons, each one arriving after the last with a Technicolor flourish. Landing in Arizona was like landing on the moon: It was hot and dry, and this was what was supposed to be so good for my dad's heart. But everything in Arizona was the same khaki-colored brown. Except, of course, for the endless, cloudless blue sky. And, I was soon to find out, it never changed. Arizona had just one hot, bright season, which just never felt right to me.

New state. New weather. New school. New home life. New every-thing. The only saving grace for me was that I had a cousin in Phoenix, Tammy. She was just a year or so older than me, and being around her was the only thing that felt even the slightest bit familiar during the fleeting and disorienting but supertransformative years I had to spend there. If I were to ask her now, Tammy would probably say I was okay to be around, but I know that I was so lost, so needy, that I would try to attach myself to her like Velcro. But she had her own scene going on, and she had a settled bunch of friends and parties to go to and all sorts of activities that she was committed to, and so I never got to see enough of her. I was just young enough that I was much more of a pest than a pal to her, I'm sure.

When I wasn't with Tammy, I just tried really hard, probably too hard, to fit in, to pretend that I somehow belonged there. Just like it is for lots of girls around this age, this was a period when I fumbled along, taking some pretty bumpy, almost jarring, tentative steps out of my childhood and into early adolescence. It was a time of massive preteen confusion, combined with a complete sense of dislocation and isolation. Man, who knew twelve could be so rugged? Who knew it could be so chokingly lonely?

My parents bought a house in what was supposed to be something of an equestrian neighborhood, in this kooky suburban development that was about five square miles and which was made up of cookie-cutter houses lined up along tidy—but tiny—lots. All of the people who lived there pretended they had a lot more space than they did, and crammed all sorts of large animals into their almost comically small backyards. I know my parents picked this part of town in a well-meaning attempt to replicate, as best they could, our old farm life. Crisscrossing this faux-strip-mall version of ranch country were these trails that looped all around the neighborhood, so I did what I always did back on the farm in Illinois: I'd go out and ride my horse, which, when I was twelve, was a palomino named Golden Boy Jet. Poor GBJ, as I called him, bristled and bridled at not having any space to let it rip and run (that's what the Jet in his name was for). It was so trippy to be riding my horse while cars zoomed by, and then to actually have to wait on a traffic light before we could cross the street. Traffic was something absolutely new to both me and GBJ, and it just added to the inescapable feeling that I'd landed on a strange, alien planet that was known by all the indifferent humans who lived there as Glendale, Arizona.

It kind of goes without saying that I figured out pretty quickly that we just weren't in Kansas—er, Illinois—anymore. And there is one incident that really crossed the "t" on this fact.

One day, while I was out riding GBJ and we were making the trail loop and heading for home, a man stepped out from behind a giant bush and exposed himself—this was the real deal, full-monty, something-is-seriously-wrong-with-this-guy brand of flashing. I mean, really? I had never seen actual man parts in living color before, and I don't think I'd ever even seen them in a book at that point! I gasped, looked away (*Gross!*), and kicked GBJ hard. Finally, he did what he loved to do best and he *ran*. That horse ran all out, ignoring every speed bump, yield sign, and stoplight in his way. He ran all the way to my parents' house without slowing down for a moment. I remember getting off of him, my legs shaking, tears welling up in my eyes, and being so freaked out that I just hurried through my routine with him, got him into his stall, and ran into the house and to my room. What upset me the most, at first, was that I knew that riding a horse in this strange city as a preteen girl wasn't something I would ever be able to do again. No, this weird suburb was not my family farm, which was big and private and safe because it was buffered by acres and acres of private land, which was surrounded by miles and miles of more private land. This was the big, bad city, where nobody was safe, especially a girl who just wished she could go home.

I stopped riding immediately.

I didn't tell my parents or anyone else about what had happened, and I pretty much shoved it to the farthest corner of my mental vault until much later in my life. I do know that, at the time, I felt embarrassed and oddly ashamed that this had happened, as though, in some way or another, I'd asked for it just by having the audacity to feel safe in a strange place. Like too many young girls do, I figured that, just because this whack job was a grown-up, he somehow had the right to do this kind of creepy stuff and I was powerless to stop him.

What?

As the mother of three girls—one now a full-fledged teen, another on the cusp of teendom, and one, mercifully, still pretty little—I mean . . . hello! How could I ever have believed that that incident was in any way possibly my fault? Even for a nanosecond? God, I just get angrier and angrier when I think about it now. Of course, I hope this kind of thing never happens to my girls, but statistics say it likely will, so, in the awful eventuality that they find themselves faced with a dude who cannot control himself, I will teach them to shout, punch, kick, scream, call out, or tell faster than GBJ got us out of there. I do not know why it's taken me becoming a mother myself to feel this kind of fierce protectiveness—toward my own girls and toward my poor younger, supernaive self, but I'm there now and it's a good, good thing.

But back then, I felt like I was the only person this had ever happened to. It wasn't until pretty recently, when, I think, I was reading one of Chelsea Handler's books, and she mentioned that this same kind of disgusting thing had happened to her, that I realized that at least I wasn't the only one. In the end, having to see Mr. Small Dick on the horse trail was the worst kind of sexual abuse I had to confront, and I know I'm very lucky for this. Way, way too many girls have it much worse.

So I gave up horseback riding, which was, for me, just like riding a bike—it was the most natural thing in the world, and the thing I most loved to do. I couldn't hide out in my room for the rest of my life, so I started to randomly patch in other things, ridiculous activities that would signal to the world, and hopefully to me, that I was actually okay, like making the cheerleading squad in seventh grade. This turned out to be dangerous in its own way, because, as the new girl on the squad, I got branded as a "stuck-up bitch" by a tough cheerleader from the other side of the tracks, the ringleader, so to speak, who managed to get all the girls to align with her. I cannot for the life of me remember that girl's name, but she decided immediately that it was absolutely necessary to kick my ass. When the moment actually came and she called me out, I just gave it right back to her and . . . it was on!

This was during lunch recess, and we upperclassmen (this was middle school, remember) were all hanging out by the monkey bars. Miss Head Cheerleader got all up in my face and so I got all up in hers. There was a little bit of slapping and name-calling (have you ever heard two thirteen-year-old girls swear?), and of course I was in a dress and a pair of ridiculous grown-up shoes. (We were all trying to be mature, and so we would wear heels to middle school. It was just so . . . pathetic.) Despite being in absolutely the wrong wardrobe for a schoolyard brawl, I didn't back down. And I even did my fair share of hitting and hair-pulling. Most important, I didn't give up. Now, on top of being known as a "stuck-up" cheerleader, I also became known as a "tough" girl, and neither of these labels helped me to feel more settled or popular. I mean, where was my big sister Cammie in her badass El Camino when I needed her? Middle school, there is no doubt, is its own ring of hell. At least it was for me.

On top of all this drama at school, there was a quieter drama brewing in my very own home.

My dad had been struggling ever since his heart attack to find his footing. All those years ago, recovering from quadruple bypass surgery was, it seems to me, a much bigger deal than it is now. It seemed like my dad had to start all over again—on every single level—and now here he was, over fifty with a bad heart, and he needed a job; he needed one soon. It was terrible to know that my already weakened dad was now facing life as a newbie, just like me. We were both trying to pull ourselves out of our separate, but equally deep and mucky ditches.

Before his heart attack, my dad had been pretty heroic in his life, and I'm not saying this from the vantage point of an adoring daughter who couldn't find any fault with her daddy. He was actually a really accomplished person and had been hugely instrumental in establishing and running the adult-education program in the greater Champaign/Urbana region of Illinois. He even founded and ran a school for low-income adults, providing them with an opportunity to learn to read and gain literacy so that they could improve their circumstances and earn more and parent better. When he'd come home from work, he'd bale hay, tend to the animals, rebuild car engines, and keep a pretty substantial family farm running. He was big and strong and charming and funny and able to lift me, throw me in the air, then catch me with ease, in his fuzzy golden arms. After the heart attack, he could barely catch his breath, let alone me. He became, almost overnight, a completely different man, not just physically, but emotionally, too. He became less demonstrative, less voluble, as though he didn't trust that he'd have enough energy for even this kind of effort. The transformation in him was remarkable—and devastating for me. I've often considered this the first time I ever felt "abandoned" by an important man in my life—the most important man in my life. Of course, this was in no way his fault—and I never blamed him—but the loss really did a number on me. Sorry, Dad.

So here we were—here he was—trying to figure out how to make a living in this strange new place, and my mom was doing the same, and they were both just as dislocated as I was. They'd had to let go of so much (their home, their older children, their incomes), and the toll that must have been taking on their marriage was way more than my prepubescent mind could process and . . . so . . .

At some point in those lost Arizona years my dad moved out of Glendale and up to a tiny patch of barren land in Prescott Valley, Arizona. I guess this was an attempt on his part to go back to the land, to go back to a lifestyle that made more sense to him. GBJ and the rest of our animals were shipped up to his place, and I'm sure this brought him comfort and a sense of purpose. At least he was away from the traffic (and the flashers!) and an education system that couldn't find a place for him. I know he was just trying to keep an important part of our heritage intact, to keep a way of life that had been so good for our family alive, however nominally. I think he wanted to find a way to keep things from changing too much, to keep things from slipping away from him, and I understand this, I do, because I've done this in my own life, too. I finally get this about him, and I totally respect it. He just wanted to keep the best of us, the best of the Garths, alive to the best of his ability.

But my parents never did explain that separation to me, and all I can really remember about it is that I would go up to my dad's place on weekends to spend time with him and to visit the animals, including GBJ. I was a restless, more than slightly dazed and confused teen, and so I'd be bored out of my mind up there, itching for something, anything, but who knew what? I look back now and regret that I'd whine to my dad about how boring it was to be there with him. I wish I could take all of that petulance and restlessness and put a lid on it. I'd go back and take one of those long drives we'd take in his battered little pickup truck, when we'd drive through the mountains of that valley, two strangers in a strange land, trying to chart our course.

Maybe I'd even tell him that I was scared and lonely, and that I missed Cammie and my other brothers and sisters, and that I didn't understand why we had left home. But if I couldn't, because I'd become too shy, too hesitant, then at least I'd ride along beside him and let myself feel settled and secure just because he was right there, driving me around in his old truck. If I could do it all over again, I'd let myself ride along beside my dear, sweet dad and just "be."

Back in Glendale, my mom and I, now on our own, left that house in the weird "farm" suburb and moved into a condo in town, and after trying her hand at selling various products like vitamins or insurance through one kind of pyramid scheme or another, she got her real estate license and started selling houses.

Meanwhile, I made it through that middle school (which was, if I recall correctly, on the campus of Sunburst Elementary School) and started high school. Seemingly overnight, there were strange new things in my life, like eyeliner and boys, and, most important, big hair. It was the eighties, after all, and so I had frizzy, ridiculous yellow hair, a young girl's version of badass makeup, and suburban mall semislutty clothes. I now looked like every other girl at that school, which was exactly what I was aiming for. I honestly didn't give any of these things any real thought; I just desperately wanted to look like everyone else and fit in, so I could fade into the background. At the same time, I threw myself into a whole bunch of socially acceptable activities in an effort to feel more connected, to act as if I somehow belonged.

There was a dance studio right near our condo, and so I started taking dance classes. I began to spend time there even when I didn't have class, because I liked the teacher so much. She would let me help out with some chores around the studio, and as I progressed through her classes, I even began to take on some teaching myself, assisting her with the very little girls in beginning tap and beginning ballet. This was, for sure, the most fulfilling part of my Arizona life.

I also—for some inexplicable reason—got a modeling card at this time. There was a strip-mall modeling school there, a franchise with a vaguely European-sounding modeling entrepreneur's name attached to it. I think my mom thought it would be a good mother-daughter activity, or maybe she was growing concerned as to what had happened to her once sweet, forthcoming little girl. So she enrolled me in the school, where I learned how to walk prettily, apply makeup in an inoffensive way, interview, go on casting calls, take a head shot, and all the seemingly important things that would put a nice polish on that perfect life of mine.

Pretty soon, I started modeling locally. One of my first jobs was for a band uniform catalog. Those uniforms were made out of the weirdest polyester blend and looked sort of like they could have been designed as the flight-attendant uniforms of a third-rate Mormon-run airline. But you know what? This was a real job, and I was getting paid (a tiny amount, but how many kids my age were making money?), and I took it all very seriously. I showed up, put on one of those itchy, hideous band uniforms, and smiled like crazy. I did everything in my power to make those band uniforms look *hot*. I wanted to do a good job, so I was never late, and I was always polite. I wanted to help my parents as best I could, because they were both struggling. In the end, these first jobs were baby steps toward my future.

CINDERELLA IN THE DESERT

When I was fourteen and a freshman in high school, I heard about some beauty-pageant/talent-show scholarship thing. I honestly cannot remember how I caught wind of it; my mom seems to recall that I was drafted into going by the mothers of my young dance school charges. Since they wouldn't be allowed backstage, they'd feel better knowing I was there, tending to their little darlings. It wasn't something I sought out, and it wasn't something I had ever dreamed about doing; that's for sure. There was the scholarship, for the winner, which was meant to encourage her to deepen her pursuit of her chosen talent, and I liked the idea of that, seeing that I aspired to be a professional dancer back in those days. But despite these pluses, at first I said no. My mom, however, coaxed me into it, appealing to the girlie side of me, convincing me that it would be fun to dress up and wear makeup and heels, and hey, I couldn't argue with that. Plus, if I actually could win that money . . . it would be so great if I could pay my own way some and give my parents a break. So I went ahead and signed on.

What was that pageant like, you ask? It was like a suburban fantasy miniversion of the whole Miss America thing. I wore a big, shiny, satiny blue dress, big hair, lots of makeup. When it came to the talent part, I put on a leotard and flitted around the stage doing some kind of lame version of modern dance while my chosen music was played on a boom box. When I watch the video of that performance now, I can see that there was some kind of divine intervention at play, some force that kept me from trying to make a go of it as a professional dancer. But you know what? I was able to speak when interviewed, and I didn't fall during my dance routine, so in the end, I felt pretty good about it all. The crazy thing is, when they announced the winner, they called my name. I made my way to the stage and a crown was placed on my head. It was all pretty strange.

What I didn't realize was that winning that pageant, my first, meant I was expected to attend the state-level pageant and do it all over again. That was the only thing about winning I did not like.

I really did not want to do another pageant. In fact, I was so not into it that I told my mom I was more than happy to let the runner-up from that first pageant take my place. My mom had other plans. She'd already read through the long-weekend itinerary, and so she kept ignoring me and instead went on about how fun it was going to be, how it would be like summer camp, but a girlie summer camp, and again, that did it: Now I was a bit . . . intrigued. There would be makeup lessons and shopping excursions. It was going to be quite the big deal over there in Bullhead City, Arizona, where it was to be held.

My mom thought it would also give us some much-needed mother-daughter time, because since we'd landed in Arizona, I'd become even quieter and more withdrawn than I had ever been before. She pointed out that the runner-up from the Phoenix pageant would actually already be there, too, in the all-important role as the first alternate, so see? I would already know one of the other girls, and since we'd all be staying in the same hotel, it was just going to be a blast! The emphasis was all my mom's, of course: Anybody who knows me has trouble imagining me joining up happily for this kind of thing. Ever.

But what else was going on in my life? Not enough to make me say no, apparently, so off we went to Bullhead City.

Once I got there, I surprised even myself and jumped right into the whole thing. I have to be honest: It was kind of fun being in this hotel with other girls my age, who, by and large, were also pretty clueless as to what they were doing there. Rehearsing the big group dance numbers was really fun, and there was great food and candy, and the whole thing just felt so luxurious for someone who had never stayed in a hotel before. I had traveled around a lot with my family back in Illinois, but that was in the "Pink Zimmer," our family's bubblegum-pink mobile home, which was, I must say, still the most fun place to spend a vacation.

I mean, this whole pageant world was the first organized fun I'd had in such a long time, if ever. I didn't feel any pressure at all, in terms of the "competition"; I just liked being in an air-conditioned wonderland that had a pool and room service, and where my mom and I were treated really well. It wasn't so bad.

When all was said and done, the girl who won belted out "New York, New York" like she'd been singing it in smoky bars all her life. She really brought the house down. She was also one of the few girls who had grown up in the pageant system, and she had one of those terrifying tiara mothers who makes you instinctively take a step or two back. I came in a respectable fourth, which meant I didn't suck, and which—more important—also meant that I would never have to do this again.

At the end of this whole experience, just as I was making a beeline for the door, one of the judges, a man named Randy James, whom I now affectionately call "Mr. Showbiz," approached my mother when I was out of earshot.

Now, I have to stop here and say that Randy is in no way one of those creepy guys who lurks around pageants looking for some kind of trouble. In fact, he was the opposite of that. He—like me—had not even really signed up for this at all; he'd been drafted into it, just as I had. His former boss, a big casting director at ABC television in New York, had been signed up to go, but at the last minute he couldn't, so he asked Randy if he'd take his place. Since the man was an old friend and colleague, Randy agreed, not only because he was a good guy, but because it would also give him a weekend away with his new bride, Kelle.

Randy had only recently, at that point, moved to LA to start his own talent agency, and it was Kelle, Mrs. Showbiz, who had pressed him to approach my mother and me.

So we did meet Randy, and I liked him. And I liked Kelle, too. He handed me a stack of index cards, what he called "sides" (short, specific script scenes that are used in auditions), and then he asked me if I'd memorize them and come back and read them for him the next morning at breakfast, before we all left for home.

I found myself saying, "Sure," only because Randy and Kelle were so great, so nice, so . . . normal.

So we went down to breakfast on our last morning in Bullhead City and I went and sat with Kelle and went through my lines with her while Randy and my mother talked about the "business." This was my first experience acting, if that's what you want to call it, and when Kelle thought we'd read through the sides enough, I went and sat with Randy and we ran through them again. When I was finished, he told my mother, "Your daughter is the only girl here who could have a career in film and television." When she told me this, after we'd checked out and were driving back to Phoenix, we laughed and laughed. We thought it was the most hilarious, most ludicrous thing we'd ever heard.

My mother also told me that they'd talked a little bit about what it took to work in Hollywood, but she had told Randy, in no uncertain terms, that she didn't understand how I could work if I didn't drive yet, hadn't even been out on a date yet. She just found the whole notion of me somehow getting work in show business to be preposterous relative to where I was in my life; I was a young fourteen, still knee-deep in childhood in so many ways. She knew how terribly shy I was, and there was no doubt, despite the fact that we hadn't communicated well with each other since our move, that I was still her little girl.

LEAVING ARIZONA

My nondescript life in Arizona went on. I honestly wish I could remember more of this time, but it's one of those periods in my life that I've just kind of blocked out because it was such a time of crushing loneliness for me.

My mother told Randy she'd look into finding me an acting coach, which she did right away through the John Casablancas Modeling and Career Center, where I'd gotten my modeling card. Randy sent audition materials to me, and I began working with a woman named Jean Fowler, a Phoenix-based acting coach. Jean would videotape me reading and send the tapes to Randy, who would then call from LA and offer feedback on my work. Then he would call and encourage my mom to encourage me. To say that Randy was encouraging, if you ask my mother, is an understatement: She would describe him as having been persistent. He said that I had "something," and he clearly did not want whatever that something was to go to waste. And so in between going to school, taking dance lessons, and working at a clothing shop in the mall called On the Move, I was beginning to learn the basics of television acting 101.

My parents were supportive of me and my acting classes, and my mom was now in regular contact with Mr. Showbiz, who wanted to know when I was going to come out to LA.

I think I was fifteen when my mom and I did go out there for a quick visit. We wanted to see the sights: Rodeo Drive, Universal Studios, the beach, and, especially for me, the ocean. We met with Randy and we ran around like tourists and then we came home. We kept sending my acting tapes to Randy, and then one day, at the start of my junior year, I told my mom and dad that I was ready to make the leap: I wanted to go to LA and give it a shot. But here's the truth of what was going on: I was miserable. I was a good student, but I was lonely as hell. I felt directionless, like I was fading away in that hot Arizona sun, and I didn't want to just die in those bright but dreary suburbs. I wanted something more. So we talked about this as a family, and the first order of business was getting my dad out to LA to meet Randy and find out what his intentions toward me were, what he had in mind when he talked about my working in Hollywood.

Well, my dad really liked Randy, and he felt that he was a good and honorable man and that he clearly wouldn't steer me wrong. The only problem my dad had with the idea of my moving out to LA was LA itself: He just didn't like it. At all. And he said that under no circumstances was he willing to move there.

My mom had saved some money, enough, she told me, if I knew I really wanted this, for us to go out there together and try it out for twelve months. That was it: She'd give it one year. At the end of that time, we would come home. I think she needed to frame it this way for both of us, so that it didn't feel like we were just jumping off a cliff. I understood the wisdom in this, and I, too, felt the only way I could do it was to think of it as "just giving it a try." Plus, we would be leaving my dad behind, and that, certainly, could never, ever be permanent.

My dad was pretty well planted by now, up there on his little parcel of land, surrounded by our animals. And my sisters Wendy and Lisa were still living near there, so my mom and I felt comfortable leaving him, knowing he was in good hands. Plus, California was just one state over, and the plane ride between Phoenix and LA was a short hop of an hour. With all of our ducks in a row, my mom and I decided to move to LA and see if I could make a go of it.

I was just sixteen when we landed in LA, and the first thing we did was go to North Hollywood High, so that I could enroll in school. Well, I walked into that place, which was tough and big, and I knew, without a doubt, that I would get my blond butt kicked back to Arizona if I were to go there, so before I was even out the door with the enrollment forms in hand, I was in tears. By the time I got back to the car, I was a sobbing mess. I couldn't do it. There was no way that I could be the new girl, not again. I had done a masterful job of making it look easy when I was a few years younger, but in all honesty, trying to make friends and fit in had nearly done me in. I knew private school wasn't an option, since my mom and I would be living on a pretty slim shoestring as it was. We sort of went through the motions of looking into some of the alternative educational options available to working kids in LA, but in the end, we decided that I'd take my high school equivalency exam, and so I went to a high school downtown on a Saturday, took a test, and that was it: a couple of weeks later, a "diploma" with my name on it came in the mail, and at least as far as the state of California was concerned, I was now a high school graduate.

I was so, so lucky, because right away I got to work. This was back in the days before GPS or Google Maps, and so my mother would drive and I rode in the passenger seat, a gigantic paperback book called the *Thomas Guide* open on my lap. The *Thomas Guide* was an encyclopedic collection of very detailed street maps, and while my mother drove, I navigated us around LA. We had no clue where we were going most of the time, and we'd usually get there just in the nick of time, and my mother would pull up to wherever the audition was, drop me off, and then wait in the car while I did my thing. Then I'd hop back into the car and pick up the *Thomas Guide*, and we'd wind our way back to our tiny apartment. I waitressed during the day and took acting classes at night, and I went to a lot of auditions and got a lot of callbacks, and within four months I had my first acting gig, a onetime guest part on the hit sitcom *Growing Pains*. My role was that of the bimbo, the girl who just shows up in a short skirt wearing lots of lip gloss. I had one speaking line, and I had to say it from the backseat of a convertible when the car I was in pulled up alongside the boy stars of the show. My line, if I recall correctly, sounds much racier now than it did when I was a goofy sixteen-year-old. It was "Sticky, sticky, sticky." And it was said in response to something like one of the boys spilling a soda on himself. I remember, even then, feeling like this bit part was slightly degrading, but I did it, knowing that it would add to my résumé in important ways. Mercifully, this was one of the only times I had to play the truly dumb blonde.

I was now a working actor, and because of this, I needed to file for legal emancipation, so I could work a full day, collect a grown-up paycheck and pay my grown-up taxes.

So I filed the petition for emancipation, and I became an adult in the eyes of the state of California, at least on paper; it's pretty amazing what a little paperwork can do for you, isn't it?

And then I got my SAG (Screen Actors Guild) card and so I was able to get health benefits, and pretty soon I had my first major part on a new show.

Now that I was actually getting a steady paycheck, I rented my first apartment in Sherman Oaks, and my mom and I moved in there. She was shuttling back and forth between LA and my dad in Arizona, and I was either working or hanging out on my own. I was super lucky to make one really great, lifelong friend, a young actress named Patrice, whose day job was managing our apartment complex. Patrice lived downstairs from me, and almost immediately we started doing things for each other, like checking in to see if the other needed anything at the grocery store, or, when my acting work began to pick up, Patrice would look after my little dog, Sasha. To kill time and keep the loneliness at bay, I began baking—a lot. I'd make cookies or cupcakes, and as soon as they were ready, I'd bring some down to Patrice. Patrice had grown up in LA, and so she had that relaxed, easy vibe of someone who knows where she is; I loved this about her. Plus, she's also from the blond tribe, and so we had that in common. We were like Ethel and Lucy, just walking into each other's places and helping ourselves to whatever was in the fridge, or racing up and down the stairs to share news that needed immediate sharing. Plus, we could be stupid and silly and hilarious together. We are still close, so very close that I feel like her kids are my kids and my kids are hers: We've definitely got that "it takes a village" thing down. As I write this, I'm getting ready to travel across the country for Patrice's wedding, a special moment I wouldn't miss for anything in the world.

After just a few short months in LA, I felt more settled, more alive, more real, and definitely more productive than I ever had in Arizona. Maybe this was going to work out. Maybe, just maybe, this was where I was meant to be.

I MISS GOING TO SWITZERLAND

When I first came to Hollywood, where everything was new and exciting, my mind developed a very clever technique for dealing with all of the industry stress and pressure that my young and naive sixteen-year-old self found herself steeped in. I affectionately thought of this little mental trick as "going to Switzerland."

Here I was, a kid who had dropped out of high school and was barely old enough to drive, but I had a manager and an agent. I was running all around LA to auditions, which led to high-stress callbacks, and I had bills of my own that had to be paid, and schedules that had to be kept.

All of this was utterly new to me; it was all about head down full immersion, about observing and listening and not letting the over-whelming *newness* of it get to me. But I think I was really overwhelmed by it all.

So I would be in, say, a meeting with a director or a casting agent or someone else important in the business, and the stakes would seem incredibly, unimaginably high, especially to my young, very excitable mind, and then—poof!—without warning or any effort on my part, smack in the middle of a very crucial point in the meeting, I'd go on a little mental vacation to this incredibly serene, yet barren place that I immediately thought of as Switzerland. In the spirit of full disclosure, I have to say that I have never, to this day, visited the real country of Switzerland, and I have no doubt that it is nothing at all like the Switzerland in my mind, because my Switzerland certainly did not have any Alps; in fact, I don't know if my Switzerland even had an outdoors. Let me explain:

My "Switzerland" was a dream version of an all-white room that had no doors, no windows, no furniture, nothing. It was a safe place. A bright and warm place. It was an empty space devoid of judgment, stress, pressure, words, or sound. My mind would just simply drift off to this magical land, and when it did, I would feel awash in a deep sense of calm. I *loved* it there.

But there was one problem. "Switzerland" was very, very far away from Hollywood—and whatever conversation I was actually involved in would get a little . . . awkward. Just as I would be drifting off comfortably, I'd hear the other person's voice from afar, calling me back to his or her world, and so just as quickly as I'd departed for Switzerland, I'd be arriving back in the real world, the person in front of me looking at me quizzically, waiting for me to pick up my piece of the conversation and reply. The following exchange was typical back then:

Important person: "Jennie? Are you with me?"

Me: "Oh. Sorry. I was in Switzerland. Where were we?"

Yes, people would look at me like I was crazy, but only for a split second, because all of this would transpire in the blink of an eye: I would check out for a quick, restorative retreat in my winter-white mental ashram, while whoever I was speaking with would carry on for both of us. Then I'd pop back in, somehow pick up my end of the thread, and we'd be back on track.

I mean, this wasn't some kind of *I Dream of Jeannie* trick, where I'd cross my arms, nod my head, and teleport, though, come to think of it, I really wish I could visit Jeannie's plush little harem bottle; that seems like a pretty sweet place to take a little mental vacation, too. The problem was, I had no control over when I'd be packing my bags and heading overseas.

So, more often than I'd like to admit, I'd find myself traveling "abroad" just when someone was saying something crucially important. I would be off in another time zone, so to speak, and though I'd be able to hear a voice reaching out from the nether regions of my mind, there would always be a slight delay in my ability to respond, so more times than I care to admit, I'd have to ask someone powerful to repeat what he or she had just said. Mr. Showbiz can certainly attest to this, and, during those early years, he became adept at covering for me by chiming in when he saw that I was zoning out.

The benefits of going off to Switzerland were not just internal. There is a lot of humility in learning to say, "Would you mind repeating that?" especially in a town where everyone talks fast and wants an answer *now*. It's pretty hard to believe that I've had any kind of career at all, given that this is such a *now* town, and *now* has never, ever been my strong suit.

The truth is, I'm one of those people who needs a moment, or ten, or maybe a week to process things, especially whatever it is you just said. There's a noticeable delay for me between when I hear your words and when they actually sink in and register in my brain, and unfortunately that delay usually causes me a lot of embarrassment, and causes the person I'm with unnecessary stress. Maybe it's a blonde thing. I don't know, but it's a bit like the sign that used to be up in the London Tube stations that warned you to mind the gap. This is the mantra of my life.

I spend a lot of time minding my gap.

And here's the thing with my gap: When I used to get stressed out, it got bigger, and bigger, and . . . eventually I would just tumble into it and fall through it and find myself plunked down in my own private Switzerland. Yay!

But this doesn't happen anymore.

I just don't go to Switzerland anymore. And I don't know why. For a good solid five or six years very early in my life, throughout my relationships with various boyfriends, two husbands, my work colleagues, my family—and even Mr. Showbiz—I would just go off to Switzerland all the time. But one day, it just stopped. My mind just stopped going there. It's not like I went to therapy to figure out how to jump-start this mental flatlining. On the contrary: I *liked* going to Switzerland, and I was really, really sad when my mind just stopped taking me there.

To this day I miss it. I do. I miss my winter-white brain vacations. A lot.

Maybe it's no coincidence, then, that my bedroom is all white: the furniture, the bedding, the walls. It's all soothing, blank white. I even recently finished a painting . . . of nothing. It's just all white.

Maybe this means that I haven't left Switzerland after all.

I WAS A TEENAGE TV STAR

Being on a successful television series like *Beverly Hills, 90210* seems like a dream come true, right? In so many ways, it truly is. First of all, it is really good money—money on a level that I just didn't understand when I was just a teenager. But I did understand that it took a ton of financial pressure off of my family, and this felt good. All of a sudden I was able to buy things for the people I loved, to send presents and treat people to dinners. I was able to support myself and become financially independent at a young age. So there was that.

And then there is the piece of getting to work with and learn from incredibly talented people, in many different fields. The crews who run a successful television show? They just may be the hardest-working, most patient people on the planet. There are the studio executives, who all have brains that move at the speed of sound. And then there are the other actors, who have also lucked out and now find themselves doing what they love. For a girl who was so miserable in high school, I can't imagine a better scenario.

And the best part of being an actress? Bringing joy to others. Making people laugh. Being able to move people, to help them escape, even for an hour or so, their own problems in life. Honestly, that part is and always has been better than even the generous paycheck.

But, of course, as with any success, there are downsides too. Success, and in particular celebrity, seems to come out of nowhere, and it hits you hard, like a runaway train. One day you're just a normal girl from the Midwest; the next, you are on the cover of a magazine and people are stopping you on the street and shaking your hand and asking for autographs. It is just, hands down, the weirdest thing you can imagine, and it can mess you up if you don't put it into perspective pretty quickly.

But I'm getting ahead of myself. When I landed the role of Kelly Taylor on *Beverly Hills, 90210*, I had been in LA just shy of a year. I had a little tiny bit of television work under my belt, but not much. Just enough that some good things had started happening for me: As I mentioned, I got my SAG card—and so health insurance—after uttering that one line on camera in an episode of *Growing Pains*. I'd also been in a TV movie for Disney called *Teen Angel Returns*, which, crazily enough, starred a little-known Canadian actor named Jason Priestley, who would soon become my costar on *90210*.

But before all that happened, my first lucky break came when I was hired to play Barbara Eden's daughter in a new series called *A Brand New Life*, which also starred the dashing Don Murray.

For a kid like me from rural Illinois, working with these legendary actors was such a stroke of great good luck. Don had been an acclaimed actor for a very long time, but the one movie he'd done that just cemented his standing as a legend for me was *Bus Stop*. He starred alongside Marilyn Monroe, a woman I have always had mad respect for. Of course, there's the blondeness and the slightly similar experience of having come up from modest means, but I mean, come on: her power, her fierce intelligence, her ability to hold up in an often completely unforgiving man's world. I had stars in my eyes when I met Don, because I really did hope that some of that Monroe magic would rub off on me, simply because of my proximity to him. I guess I was hoping for some kind of "six degrees of Kevin Bacon" magic to happen, and that somehow I'd be transformed. A girl can dream, right?

And then there was the incomparable Barbara Eden. I mean, she was Jeannie, for God's sake! She knew I was new to all of this acting business, and so she took me under her wing and taught me about being professional and prepared. I sat on set and watched her like a hawk, I mean literally studied her every move. From Barbara I learned about set etiquette, and how to hit your mark every time. She taught me how powerful yet soft a woman could be in this industry. She was incredibly kind and mentoring, and I remember being devastated when the show was canceled after only seven episodes, because over those few short months, I'd grown incredibly fond of and close to Barbara and Don and the rest of the cast and crew, all of whom had become my work family. I knew that, without being able to see them every day, I would be somewhat lost and adrift in this big, strange city, and I dreaded it.

But I kept my head down and my eyes on the prize. I kept myself very busy working as a waitress, going on tons of auditions, and continuing to take acting classes at night. I was, I suppose, living the Hollywood version of being in college, because I was doing what any aspiring young actress needed to do. I had one year, just twelve months, to give it my all, and if things didn't pan out, I'd likely go back to Arizona—or, even better, Illinois—and get on with my life. All I had at that point was my determination. And, of course, Mr. Showbiz, who always manages to come through just when I need him most.

And this was never truer than when it came to landing me an audition for a new teenage drama that was being cast the year I turned seventeen. There was a ton of buzz surrounding this project, because it was the brainchild of the legendary producer Aaron Spelling, who had produced such television megahits as *Charlie's Angels*, *The Mod Squad*, *Dynasty*, and *The Love Boat*, just to name a few. But it had been a while since he'd hit it big. Mr. Spelling was due for a comeback, and I wanted in on it—just like every other kid in town—including, I later learned, my dear friend Patrice.

When the casting call for *90210* went out, Mr. Showbiz did his thing and sent over my head shots, and we heard pretty quickly that these had been thrown out, likely before they'd ever even reached the casting directors. It was clear that only seasoned actors were going to be considered for this project, but Mr. Showbiz, who'd had a long and profitable relationship with Spelling's team when he was a casting director for ABC in New York, persisted, and somehow managed to finagle a meeting for me with Mr. Spelling himself.

I'll never forget that day when I walked into the ultra chic Spelling offices, a suite of rooms with thick, luxurious shag carpeting, plush couches, and occasional tables that had candy dishes filled with cigarettes on them.

Mr. Spelling greeted me as though he'd known me my whole life. He was very warm, very wonderful, very huggy. With his infamous hunched-over posture, he spoke to me in a tone of pride and encouragement that immediately set me at ease; then he escorted me into a room full of executives and I read for them. When I was finished, Mr. Spelling smiled and began to say incredibly complimentary things, while the other executives just nodded in agreement. They all stood, we shook hands, and I left. It seemed to be over before it had even started, and I remember just being so nervous when it was all over. I left the conference room, met up with Mr. Showbiz, and as we were leaving the building and making our way across the parking lot, for some inexplicable reason I turned back to look up at Mr. Spelling's offices and there he was, standing in the window, giving me a big old double thumbs-up. I guessed that meant I'd done all right. To this day I can see still Aaron's smiling face and those thumbs.

I've heard that I was the first person he cast, but who knows? The character I would be playing was a teenager named Kelly Taylor, who was the archetypical mean girl from Beverly Hills. She was rich and spoiled and the polar opposite of me in every way, except that we were both blondes. I couldn't wait to play her. This had also been the part Patrice read for, and I was pretty stunned when I got it. She was totally excited for me and always has been, and always will be. She's something special, that one, a true friend.

The first cast read-through was held right at Mr. Spelling's house—not the gigantic mansion of legend, but the home he lived in before he built what was, for a long time, the biggest house in LA. God, I was so shy, so nervous! I kind of collapsed into one of the huge, overstuffed couches we were all perched on, and I just stared down at the script that I clutched on my lap. I couldn't help wondering what the hell I was doing there with these other actors—most of whom had a lot more experience than I did. There was Shannen Doherty, of *Heathers* fame; Ian Ziering, Jason Priestley, Tori Spelling, Gabrielle Carteris, Brian Austin Green, Carol Potter, and James Eckhouse. It was an incredibly heady moment, like being called up to the major leagues right out of high school. It was such a huge, huge day for me.

I sat there on the plush couch just hoping that I wouldn't screw up. I did not want Mr. Spelling to realize that he'd made a terrible mistake hiring me, that it had all been a misunderstanding, and would I mind getting up and leaving and never coming back? I was so thankful Jason was there, at least one familiar face, and boy, could he make you feel welcome and comfortable, with those eyes and that smile! Everyone else seemed really nice, too. I was nearly crippled with the awful wallflower angst that I've battled my whole life. When it hits, I just buckle up and get to work. So that was what I did that first day: *Eyes on the page, do your job, get the hell out!*

Despite how terrified I was, I got through that first read-through just fine, it seems, because I spent the next decade of my life on the show.

Beverly Hills, 90210 launched on the Fox network in the fall of 1990, when I was eighteen. At first it didn't get much attention, and there were even murmurings of its possibly being canceled. But then the network executives made an incredibly brilliant decision. Back in the day, summers were when networks would just roll out reruns of their most popular shows and maybe toss a made-for-TV movie or two into the mix, just to keep viewers from thinking they had just packed up and gone on hiatus for the summer (which was what everyone pretty much did). But Fox decided to do a special summer season of *Beverly Hills, 90210* and shoot new episodes so that the target demographic—kids who would be home from school all summer with nothing else to do but watch TV—would have something fresh to watch, something written and produced just for them. So we kids from fictional Beverly High also slid into the summer thing, and this one-off original summer season featured our characters on our own "summer break." Instead of roaming the halls of Beverly High, we were working our summer jobs, hitting the beach, and creating massive amounts of teen relationship drama, Southern California beach–style.

But that's not all those crafty producers had up their sleeves: They also added a "secret weapon" by bringing on a character named Dylan McKay, a bad boy who would be in town only for the summer, hanging out with his absentee businessman father. Dylan McKay, played by Luke Perry, became an overnight heartthrob. He was so wildly popular that his six-episode story arc was extended and extended and then extended some more, and he soon became a regular, full-time cast member— and one of my very closest friends.

But let's forget about Dylan for a moment and let me tell you what happened after that "bonus" summer season of the show. What happened is that all hell broke loose! In just a matter of weeks, we went from just being another generic ensemble cast of any old prime-time drama to being . . . *superstars*. (It helps to emphasize this by whispering it like Molly Shannon as Mary Katherine Gallagher on *SNL*, the insane Catholic schoolgirl.) I mean, what happened to us was nuts. It was madness! Pandemonium! Insanity! No, really, it was totally ridiculous. And utterly and completely overwhelming.

We were suddenly on the cover of every magazine, and our characters were being talked about as though they were real people. But *we* were the real people, and I don't think any of us were prepared for the stardom that was thrust upon us in this way. Thank God we had one another, because we were able to protect each other from the harm this kind of sudden fame can bring with it by staying close and huddling up and focusing on getting the job done. Maintaining our professionalism as a group protected us and kept us all somewhat sane while our lives changed forever. And it bonded us as friends for life.

I remember sometime early in season two, just after that summer season launched us into the stratosphere in terms of ratings and "Q" factor, I was sent by myself to a mall somewhere in Indiana to do an appearance. Somehow the guys who ran security for the mall didn't get the memo that the show had become a huge hit, and so about ten thousand screaming teenagers showed up and began pushing one another, trying to rush the stage. I watched, dumbfounded, as the body of a girl who had fainted was passed, mosh-pit style, up toward the stage, and then dumped right there in front of me. Mr. Showbiz was standing in the wings, working his phone, and the next thing I knew, we were surrounded by Indiana state police and I was being hustled off the stage, which, by then, was rocking back and forth. People were falling down, getting stepped on, and screaming. At one point Mr. Showbiz grabbed me by the shirt and we ran through the double doors that were behind the stage.

This kind of intense fan reaction was not something any of us had expected, especially not me. I remember feeling really bad that we'd just bolted and that I'd left all those fans in the lurch, but this was no normal meet and greet: The event made the national news, as a run-of-the-mill mall event that had turned into a riot.

And mind you, this kind of thing began happening to us before there was any kind of social media or any of the other technologies that have since spawned the outrageous (and out-of-control) cult of celebrity voyeurism we now live in. This was the kind of crazy groundswell of popularity that usually happened to rock bands, not a bunch of kids making a television show. Plus, I was really on my own now: my mother, knowing that I was well situated in Los Angeles, began to spend more and more time back in Arizona with my dad.

After that trip to the mall in Indiana, everything in my life was turned upside down. Now I couldn't go anywhere at all without being approached by strangers who wanted an autograph, a photo, or just to touch me. I had recently bought my first car, a black SUV with tinted windows and bulletproof doors, which was what the dealer told me all the young stars were driving. I had no idea how I was supposed to behave, so I just went along for the ride, doing what I was told to do, trying my best just to enjoy that crazy wave. And thank God for Patrice then, too. We would do something really off the radar, like go to a tiny nail salon for a manicure, and we'd come out, our wet hands held high, and there would be a mob of people there, a pack of paparazzi surrounding my car. Or one time, after dinner, we went to get my car out of valet parking and we literally couldn't drive off—the paparazzi just made a human wall and stood there. If Patrice hadn't been there, I don't know what I would have done.

When all the madness first hit, Mr. Spelling hired bodyguards for all of us, but this security covered us only when we were actually on set. So there I'd be, out in Van Nuys, at work, surrounded by a huge crew of people, all of whom were paid to make me and my fellow cast members look good and be safe. People were hired to shuttle us around, make sure we had enough food and water, even tell us when we could take a bathroom break. I'd be treated like the queen of Siam for twelve hours a day; then we'd wrap and I'd head home, by myself, in my big, black, bulletproof car. Then I'd get to my home, scurry into the house, and stay there, until I had to get up and do it all over again.

This was an incredibly strange way to live, even for someone who'd had a pretty isolated upbringing. I felt comfortable—almost comforted— by all of the workers buzzing around me during the day, but after hours, I'd find myself getting anxious when strangers approached me, and so simple tasks, like going to the grocery store, or the mall, or to get gas, became overwhelming exercises in having to be "on," when my natural inclination was to shut down and not interact with anyone. I was barely nineteen and began to suffer a level of anxiety that was, at times, nearly paralyzing. When the panic attacks started to kick in, I became even more withdrawn.

To say that my life was schizoid is an understatement: I'd be coddled and pampered and doted on all day; then I'd be on my own, with no one to talk to except dear Patrice. I was young, I was making an obscene amount of money, and I had no clue about any of it. All I knew to do was to keep my head down and work my ass off, because I knew that if I let any of the "star" stuff go to my head, I would be in trouble.

Looking back at those years, from when I was roughly sixteen to twenty, I think it's fair to say that landing such a plum role pretty much right out of the gate didn't help me grow up in some crucial ways. It's taken me a long time (just ask my shrink!) to really look at how that experience shaped me, and how it affected the way I conduct myself in my relationships and, consequently, what I expect from the people around me. I went from being a lonely girl to being taken care of in this weird, over-the-top way. It was trippy! It was traumatizing! And it's still trippy, and I feel very, very fortunate that it didn't screw me up more than it did.

The constant attention pushed me even more into my introversion and made me feel really overwhelmed and alone. I started spending even more time on my own, more time away from the real world, if you will. I stopped going to the movies or clothes shopping or doing any of the other things normal young people do. I would wait until well after dark and then go to a twenty-four-hour grocery store, in the hope that I could then shop without being accosted by a well-meaning but overeager fan (or two, or many). I wouldn't say that I ever stepped over the line into full-blown agoraphobia, but I would say I definitely came close, and I've been battling the anxiety that early stardom brought on ever since.

As my public life grew, my private life shrank. Being still new to town, I had very few friends, but with those I did have, I built incredibly intensely loyal friendships. It is worth noting that these few good souls are still my closest friends today. I probably hang on to people tighter than I ought to, because once you're in with me, you're in for life. I realize this makes me sound almost stalkerlike, but it's true: I'm loyal beyond belief, and sometimes certainly beyond reason. Most of my friends—actually all of my closest friends—are not in show business, and of course I have lost a few dear friends along the way. But mostly I'm just very grateful for the people who've stood by me, and for how lovingly they've helped shape my life, how they've helped me to stay grounded when it was pretty close to impossible to do so.

Becoming a teenage TV star is almost too wonderful, too over-the-top everything: It's exciting, it's fun, it's validating, it's lucrative, and it's completely life-changing. It can, if you're not careful or lucky or both, utterly ruin your life. Thank God I, and my beloved castmates, managed to make it out of all that alive.

9021-OH

I loved my job on *Beverly Hills, 90210*, and yet it wasn't as glamorous as people thought. For any of you out there who are happily delusional fans of that iconic nineties television show, I'm going to advise you to skip ahead, because I'm not going to pull any punches and I'm going to tell you what making this show was really like. So if you'd prefer not to hear the nitty-gritty, then you can just flip through the pages and meet up with us later on. I might be about to burst some big bubbles. And because I am historically such a people pleaser, I do not want to be the one who kills those *90210* fantasies of yours. However, I am writing about this notorious time in my life, and that means no sugarcoating, no sneakily whisking you, the reader, off to some fictionally enhanced version of the Peach Pit.

First reality check: We cast members—me, Jason, Ian, Luke, Shannen, Brian, Gabrielle—none of us were from Beverly Hills. Only Tori was. But even Tori's life for that decade of shooting was not at all like the seemingly glamorous one she grew up in. No, our lives were nothing like the lives of the Walsh twins and their gang of friends.

All of those mansions with the pristine lawns that flash through the show's opening montage? Those were B roll. Stock video of the mansions of Beverly Hills. Instead, picture this: You're driving down the ugliest industrial street in a town called Van Nuys, fifteen miles and a world away from the chic streets of Beverly Hills. When you get to the end of that street, turn right into a driveway that's behind a chain-link fence that is topped with curled barbed wire (hey, there's a lot of pricey film equipment on a soundstage). Once you get through the gate, slow down, so you can find your designated parking spot, which you'll recognize by the chipped number spray-painted onto one of the concrete parking blocks that neatly divide up the broken asphalt. Remember this number, because it's not only your parking space number, but it's how you will be identified on the call sheet, which is the document that is handed out to the cast and crew at the end of a day's shooting in advance of the next day's work.

Oh. And you will be coming here every day for an average of fourteen hours a day, five days a week. For the next . . . ten years.

My number was three, for a good few years. But then . . . I became number two! And eventually, before our long run was over, I did, in fact, become number one. How did this promotion happen, you ask? You move up the call sheet only when someone above you 1) gets fired, 2) quits, or 3) is sent to rehab. You can only imagine how good it felt, then, when I finally made it to number one.

Despite the fact that the number on the call sheet was not a ranking of talent or popularity or importance to the show, I have to say that, once I became number one, things did seem to lean a bit more favorably in my direction.

For instance, my dressing room for most of my years on the show was a dark, windowless cubicle the size of a closet that was next to Ian's and directly across from the bathrooms. One of the first things I bought for this space was a boom box, so I could drown out the sound of Ian on the phone (he was quite the wheeler-dealer back then and was always excited about one moneymaking scheme or another) and the never-ending flushing sound coming from the toilets across the hall.

I wanted to make this tiny closetlike room feel homey and comfortable, so I squeezed a small futon into the space, and this left about three feet of room to spare. I brought in candles and lots of pillows and blankets (once the futon was in, there wasn't enough room to accommodate a chair as well). I had the set decorators paint it various colors over the years, and for the first few, it was painted a deep, dark burgundy. Despite how crowded my sanctuary was, I loved having people over (pull up a cushion!), and I ate lunch in there almost every single day. By myself. (This was our only long break of the day, and I badly needed the quiet.) From time to time, I'd put a note on the door that said, "Please be quiet; I am sleeping," but this was never helpful, because we were, after all, a half dozen kids who were holed up here working very long days. There was a lot of yelling and running up and down that hallway, lots of being chased. Lots of roughhousing and playing. And there were also lots of fights. We were teenagers in a strange grown-up world, our hormones raging and our social lives so restricted that we were, at all times, either best friends or enemies, or both.

After a couple of years putting up with this, I began to covet the corner cubicle, but it was occupied by someone higher up the call list . . . my nemesis! Of course, this "dressing room" (if you can call it that) had been given to Shannen because she was the one of us who had landed at *90210* already a star. Her space seemed to be the only one that was out of the fray, and it was definitely roomier than mine. It was a space, an oasis, I longed for, and year after year I'd gaze down the hall and dream.

And then one day, without warning, she was gone. There was no good-bye, no nothing. One day she just wasn't on the call sheet. The set was so oddly quiet, and now the much-desired dressing room was beckoning to me. I wrapped my boom box in a blanket and scurried down the hall, checking over my shoulder to make sure no one saw me take possession of this vacant nook. By then I was out there in Van Nuys, on this soundstage (which, by the way, also happened to house a porn production company) from sunup to sundown, five days a week. It was time for me to leave my burgundy den behind. This time I was going to do my space up right!

I had my then-assistant Adele get a giant white parachute at a nearby army surplus store. I anchored this over the hideous fluorescent light fixtures that dangled from the ceiling, then tacked up the rest at the four corners of the room. Now, instead of gazing up into a dull, depressing warehouselike ceiling, I was looking at what I thought of as my billowy nylon cloud. I think this was just before my twenty-first birthday, and I was, being the late bloomer that I was, finally beginning to get a little edgier and was no longer just all about "Switzerland" at this time in my life, so I had the set designers paint the walls a glossy black. Then I disconnected the lighting. (Good-bye, ugly fluorescent glow—may I never, ever see you again!) I had created, much to the awe and jealousy of my castmates (or so I thought) a true cave. My dressing room was now the farthest from the action; it was dark and windowless and cold, and I could hide out in there and thereby bypass all the workplace drama that was going on around me twenty-four/seven. I needed this kind of isolation so that I could gather myself enough to come out of my cave, brave the world, and do my "job."

This is what a typical day looked like for me when I was working on *90210*. I would be up and out of my house by six a.m., driving the still-dark streets of the San Fernando Valley, where I lived, dressed in sweats, my hair wet. I'd be behind the wheel of my big-ass Suburban with the tinted, bulletproof windows, navigating the LA freeways long before rush hour started. I'd pull into the lot in Van Nuys and make a beeline for the makeup trailer, which was a crazy hive of activity—even at six in the morning you had to yell to be heard over the din of hair dryers and music. While you were in your makeup chair, a PA would bring you breakfast, if you wanted it. Actually, you could probably get anything you wanted delivered to you. They wouldn't have batted an eye if I'd asked for a bagel and a bump of coke, come to think of it, but I usually just had coffee. Even though the makeup trailer was always buzzing with tons of adrenaline, I was usually so tired that I'd just slump down in my chair while whoever was assigned to work on me would spackle and polish me up for the day. Once this was done, I had to go over to the hair end of the trailer to have my hair blown out.

It's important to mention how bonded an actor tends to become with his or her makeup and hair people. Speaking personally, one of my best friends to this day was my hairdresser from the original *90210* days, my Michael. He knows exactly when to make me laugh (actually, no one makes me laugh harder on this planet) and when to just chill, not to mention he always just wants to make me look my best! Who doesn't want a best friend like that?

Then it was off to wardrobe, and I'd be handed a couple of hangers with my outfits for that day's shoot. And then, with only a lunch break and a bathroom break or two, we'd get to work. Those days were long and hard, but that soundstage became my sanctuary, the only place where I could just relax and be myself.

When I took over Shannen's old dressing room I'd been with the show for six years, and by then I could no longer keep track of the string of guest actresses who were brought in to service the story line du jour and placate the male stars, too, who, I'm sure, were tired of looking at me and Shan and Tori all day, every day. The male actors who were brought in to do the same for us girls had become a blur of familiar haircuts (why did they all look like Luke or Jason?) and blazingly white teeth. I knew this was, for them, their big break, but I was so burned-out by then—and didn't even know it—that I'm certain I came across as a bitch, someone who thought she was too good for it all, but who, in fact, was just too tired for it all.

So whenever I was not on set, I would withdraw into my cave and violate all kinds of fire-safety laws and light candles under my parachute and listen to Portishead on my enormous boom box, and I'd close myself off and just . . . brood.

I was a bit of a loner. A worrier. When I think back on it, I believe it's because I was way more burned-out and overwhelmed by it all than I knew. I mean, how does a fifteen-, sixteen-, seventeen-, even twenty-year-old girl who has been working nonstop for the past five years have any concept of what the real world is like: how to have fun, goof off, or just do nothing? I was tired, yet I was also supremely grateful that I was making a living and was able to support myself and help my family. The truth is I had no reference point, no playbook to help me figure out the proper balance. All I had was the good counsel of my loving family (who were all now at least one state away, and though they loved me like mad, they really had zero concept of what my life was turning into) and the levelheaded, excellent professional guidance of Mr. Showbiz.

When I compare what I must have been like at age fifteen with what my eldest daughter is like now at the same age, I'm filled with a sense of deep compassion and even a bit of sadness for my young self and my young costars. I mean, there we were—just kids, but we weren't enrolled in Beverly Hills High or any other high school for that matter. We were isolated out in Van Nuys, on a skanky soundstage, working our asses off. I'd finish a long day, wipe off the layers of caked-on makeup, climb into my car, and go home. Then I'd get up and do it all over again.

At work, I was all about business. I always knew my lines; I always knew where I was supposed to stand; I always, without too much complaint, wore whatever the wardrobe people gave me. I adored the crew: the camera guys, the grips, the glam squad, the prop team. These people were my new family, and I wanted them to know that I took their jobs as seriously as I took mine. All of the crew was there at least fourteen hours a day, too, giving up their time in the real world as much as we were, but they weren't getting any of the perks, the accolades, or especially the ridiculous paychecks we actors were getting. I wouldn't have been able to live with myself if I had been the one holding them up by bitching about what I had to wear or complaining about how shitty I thought my hair looked. I was not going to be the one who blew the schedule because I had gotten too wasted in the "it" club of the moment the night before. It just wouldn't have been right.

So I made a decision. I made a decision about which team I was going to play for, and I chose production. I became known as a "trouper" by the producers, a professional. This choice put me at odds with some of my fellow cast members, and even felt kind of like drawing a line in the sand sometimes, and this made me seem uncool and even more uptight, in their eyes. But you know what? That was something I could live with.

Don't get me wrong: I loved my fellow castmates then, and I still love them to this day. There's not one of them whom I wouldn't drop everything for in a heartbeat. There is not one among them I wouldn't be happy to see (well, maybe there is just one, if I'm being honest)—and I do see many of them, even the ones who are supposed to be my sworn enemies.

And I like all of them, each and every one, much, much better now that we're adults, because back in the day, when we were interacting as a group, there was just always way too much fucking teenage drama. I was by no means an innocent bystander when it came to all this drama among the cast members, either. Being in that competitive, narcissistic world brought out each of our personal heavy-duty self-esteem issues, and when that happens, well, that's when drama and angst seem to thrive.

I remember one infamous "red dress" incident that exemplifies this kind of petty selfishness. We were gearing up for the seasonal promotional photo shoot, and all of us leading ladies wanted to be the one to wear the red dress that was chosen for the shoot. After all, this would be the photo that would be seen around the world for the rest of the year, and since red is a pretty eye-catching color, especially on blondes, we were each determined to wear that damn dress. Well, I put my little foot down and bitched and moaned and . . . so, in the end, there were two special stars wearing red that day. And one, not by accident, was dressed in black. Little did I know that, thanks to social media, I'd be able to see that photograph for the rest of my life, to revisit one of the brattiest, most inane days of my life. All I have to do is find that photograph and zoom in on our fresh young faces to see how pissed off Tori and I are and how completely over us the boys are. And then there's the girl in black. It's no fun to see that photo and be reminded of my petty, completely self-absorbed, younger self, but what are you going to do? I, unfortunately, was a teenager once, too.

So there were times when I added my own spice to that drama stew, but I tried to keep it to a minimum on set, because . . . let's just say I had all the drama I could handle just trying to stay afloat on my own in Hollywood.

THE RULE OF THREE

I don't know why it is, but there is a universal truth that when you put three teenage girls together, some serious shit is going to go down. I have no idea why this is true, but it is.

At least, this was true for the dynamic that played out between me, Shannen, and Tori on the set of *Beverly Hills, 90210*.

When we began the show, Shannen was the one with the most acting experience. She came to the show on the heels of reaching teen stardom in the hit movie *Heathers*, and so she strode onto that set with a level of confidence and intensity that I had never seen in anyone before, let alone a girl my age.

To say that she was strong is an understatement. A fellow Aries sister . . . she had some set of horns! She had opinions about a lot of things, including the writing, the wardrobe, you name it. And she wasn't afraid to share them, even if it meant sounding like a complete and utter bitch. She didn't care about that; she just wanted to be heard.

For her, it was all about being what she saw as professional, and she could bring a ferocious kind of energy to the set that could, at times, come across as just being difficult. I didn't understand this then, but I do now, and that's probably why Shannen and I have become so close as we've gotten older. I was fresh off the bus, just tiptoeing into Hollywood, after all. And she was seasoned, and had already dealt with an absurd amount of pressure and speculation and all the judgments that come with being a strong, confident, independent young lady. I never wanted to piss anyone off, while she seemed, from my very naive perspective, to live for pissing people off. Looking back now, I recognize how challenging it can be for an actress to be taken seriously, and I understand where she was coming from. I have a lot of compassion for young Shannen. I mean, the truth is, I have a lot of compassion for just about any girl trying to stand up and be heard out there in this big, scary world.

So yes, I found her to be intimidating, but I also loved her to death, in that way that fifteen- and sixteen-year-old girls *love* their best girlfriends: They're either as thick as thieves, sharing *everything*, or they're driving each other nuts and trying to gouge each other's eyes out.

Poor Tori, the youngest of the three of us, was, inevitably, often caught in the middle, and she was always trying to smooth things over, trying to get Shan and me off each other's backs and get along, but her efforts usually failed. She was a peacemaker, desperate for everyone to get along—and she's still like that today. Tori is such a sweet soul.

I remember toward the end of season six, shortly after Shannen had left the show, I decided to chop all of my hair off, because I just couldn't take having to go through a blowout five days a week (it felt like there were big brush-size bruises on my wrecked little scalp), and I thought that maybe if my hair didn't need so much time, I might be able to nap for fifteen minutes before we started shooting. And actually, I needed a change! I was tired of looking at that same reflection in the mirror every morning at six a.m. For about five minutes I felt liberated, but pretty quickly I realized that haircut wasn't the greatest decision.

The first day I came to set with my "new look," I ran into Tori, and I watched as she tried her hardest to compliment me. She stood there and struggled until she finally just blurted out that she hated it and it made me look "matronly." She tried to back off of this rare indiscretion by telling me that what she meant to say was that she thought it made me look forty, which it did. But back then, in my early twenties, telling me I looked forty was like telling me I looked ninety. I couldn't really be pissed at her, because I knew how much she loved me, and I loved it that she didn't want to just lie to me, like so many others obviously had by not telling me it was a god-awful haircut. Then she stepped toward me and tried to mess my hair up, and when she was finished, she stepped back and said, "There. That's a little edgier." I looked in the mirror and I felt like Carol Brady was staring back at me. She was right; it was not a good look. And for a long time after that, I was always ducking whenever Tori would come at me with those hands, wanting to mess me up, God bless her.

Back in the day, Tori and I spent a lot of time together, even though at first it was kind of weird, her being the boss's daughter and all. I didn't want to cross any professional boundaries, so I held back a little, defaulting into my usual pretty shy self. But we warmed up to each other, Tori and I, and we'd hang out in her dressing room because, like me, she didn't like to venture out of her cocoon too much, either. We became sisters of sorts. Still, to this day, there isn't much I wouldn't do for her if she needed me. We were close—except when she was hanging out with Shannen.

Ah, the rule of three.

Where Tori was easygoing, Shannen could be intense. But you know what? I could match her intensity with my stubbornness, my self-righteousness, and so while Shannen would be freaking out I'd be standing there nose-to-nose with her, my nostrils flaring, eyes glaring.

Like I said, we were both card-carrying Aries women, so . . . Tori would look from one to the other of us nervously, not at all sure how to make peace, given that either one of us could blow up at any moment.

So there we were. Sometimes I'd feel like Shannen was my best friend in the world. And often she was, and still is. I mean, how could she not be? She was one of a small handful of people whom I spent most of my time with. But there was an aspect to our closeness (for all of us, at various times, I'm sure) that was more like Stockholm syndrome than friendship, because we were holed up by contract—and not by personal choice—for years upon years upon years with one another. We didn't have the benefit of having several hundred girls our same age swirling around us on a bright, sunny high school campus, pulling us in and out of various dramas. It was just us, shut up on that dark, drab soundstage. There was no buffer for us, no way to step out of one another's sight lines long enough to cool off and grow up for a second. We were girls. We were well-meaning, often overextended, in-over-our-heads girls. And like all girls, of course, we were sweet and thoughtful and all that, but also, we could be . . . mean. I mean really eye-gougingly vicious— you don't want any piece of this mean.

One of the great *90210* legends is that Shannen and I actually came to blows one time. I will tell you that this never happened—although we did come very, very close.

If I remember correctly—and I probably don't, given the rocky terrain that is my memory—we were shooting a scene and Shannen kept grabbing at the hem of my skirt, trying to slap me on the leg—anything to get me to react and break character. Finally, when she'd pulled up my skirt, and my bare ass was exposed for everyone on the set to see, I did snap and I yelled at her, something to the effect of, "Come on, bitch! We're taking this outside!" I strode off the set and out into the dingy, crappy parking lot. Shannen was right behind me, and behind her were the rest of the cast and a lot of the crew.

We were on fire! We were both throwing "f"-bombs and insults at each other like it was World War III. It was crazy! I mean really absurd. Before we could kill each other, Luke and Jason dived into the middle of it and pulled us apart, Luke backing away, holding me tight, while I clawed and punched at the air in front of me, while Jason pushed Shannen to the other side of the parking lot.

It was ridiculous.

So we didn't actually come to blows, but that doesn't mean that, during the years that we worked so closely together, we didn't want to rip each other's heads off. What was so unbelievably strange was how this personal tension somehow bled into the relationship between our characters, and by the time Shannen left the show, there was very little love lost between us or our characters. Those of you who know the show know that Brenda and Kelly began as best friends but turned into bitter rivals, and Shannen and I did, too, at least for a time while we were working together.

We were, back then, just two immature girls who were ruled by hormones, and forced to be way too close to each other for way too many hours a day. In short, we were like oil and water—or gasoline and a match, depending on what day it was.

And yet somehow, we survived to tell the tale. We both get a kick out of it now, looking back at our young selves, those silly girls. Isn't that something? Brenda and Kelly actually did grow up, and Shannen and I did, and now I count her as one of my dearest, closest friends.

After Shan left the show, the producers brought in an actress named Tiffani Thiessen to play the new bad girl, Valerie Malone. I was so over the drama that we'd been steeped in for so long that I greeted our newcomer with the iciest, bitchiest, most off-putting demeanor possible. It took me a few months to I realize that I was unconsciously perpetuating the "rule of three" dynamic, and I realized that I just didn't want that anymore. So I went to Tiffani, apologized to her, and began again. After that, we became really close friends, too, and both Tiffani and Tori even honored me by being bridesmaids in my wedding.

It's funny, come to think of it: I have three girls myself, but the "rule of three" just doesn't apply in our house, thank God. Maybe it's because they're spread out in age, but my girls are with one another the way my sisters and I were: They're closer than close. And they love one another madly, fiercely, and protectively. Oh, they get into the usual pissy moods like all girls do, but sisterly love is the abiding vibe in our home.

Nowadays, I'd say that three is a pretty great number—lucky, even.

BEAUTIFUL BOYS

I can't write about my *90210* years without talking about the boys. Collectively, they were just about as beautiful as you can get, and once the show took off, posters of them went up on the bedroom walls of teenage girls across the land. They were mobbed by girls and women who wanted to get close to their sunny, beachy awesomeness. And who could blame them?

I adored each one of them. And still do.

There's Jason, he of the megawatt, crinkly-eyed smile. I remember he had this mullet, this kind of comedian hairdo, and it just cracked me up. He's incredibly talented, that one, and he has this ability to make everything look so easy. He sets people at ease right away. He's also pretty salty, and I remember my mom telling me to keep an eye on the guy with the potty mouth. He also smoked cigarettes back then. We'd often be hanging out outside the set in Van Nuys, having a smoke, killing time, and someone would make him laugh, which happened often.

He'd throw his head back and laugh in this beautifully disarming, delightful way that made everyone laugh right along with him. And he was such a guy, such a dude: Just give him a cigarette and a beer and he was good. He was sexy before I even knew what that was.

Then there was Ian, who had come to LA from the New York theater world. That's what struck me the most about him: that he was enthusiastic and wise and ambitious as all hell. I remember that we had to kiss in one of the earlier episodes, like right after we had met, and he asked me if we could go to the garage of this house we were shooting at "to rehearse." I didn't know what to say, so I said, "Sure," and went along. It was the most awkward situation yet . . . one little practice peck and I said, "Okay! I'm good!" Of course, I know now that you don't have to "rehearse" those kisses . . . I told you he was ambitious!

Ian is, in a word, gung ho. I don't think he's met a challenge that hasn't excited him, including, just last year, appearing with the Chippendales in Las Vegas. Shannen and I flew out to catch his once-in-a-lifetime performance, and I was bowled over by how damn buff and hot the man is—and he's pushing fifty! We had a blast, and it felt great to be around him again. I miss all that Ian energy. And that sly, sly smile.

I do have one Ian story—one that he actually loves to tell. I was dating this guy and Ian was dating some lovely young woman, and the four of us wound up in a hot tub together back at Ian's place. Someone was stroking Ian's arm and he assumed it was me, since I was sitting next to him, but after a few minutes, this hand comes up out of the water and rests on his shoulder and starts massaging his neck. He looks over at me, and at the same instant we both realize it's not my hand; it's the hand of my date! I will never, ever forget the look on Ian's face at that moment. Or how much fun he's had telling that story all these years.

And sweet Brian, the youngest and by far hippest of the group. I swear, that one started out just a boy and ended up a true hunk of a man! I watched him transform from peach-fuzz-faced, wide-eyed, and innocent, to this strong, silent, tattooed gentleman with piercing eyes and the charms and manners of a saint. Brian went through a number of phases over the course of our years working together. The one that stands out for me was when he was producing music and really starting to find his own identity amid all the commotion. The other guys would tease him about his hip-hop flair, but Brian knew what was up far more than any of us, and I always respected him for standing his ground and being true to himself in the face of their nonsense.

And then there was Luke, the mystery man who joined us for that breakout summer season as a guest star and who was so alluring and magnetic that he became a regular cast member. Whereas Jason was so personable and charming, Luke was broody and elusive. He never said a lot. He wasn't friendly. He always seemed to have a toothpick in his mouth, a ball cap pulled down low. He totally had that James Dean thing going on, you know? I never saw him reading poetry, but I imagined he would. He was the recluse. The unattainable one.

Luke's quietness appealed to me. His unfussy confidence really drew me in. We were comrades in our appreciation of silence. We connected almost instantly in a pretty deep way, but I think we both knew that our friendship needed to be just the way it was: accepted and not tampered with.

So what was I to do with all of these luscious men around me? Of course we flirted with one another—constantly! Every day on set was a flirt-fest, but it was all pretty harmless, because we all usually had romantic partners off-set. But we were young, we were holed up together, and when we weren't working, what were we to do? Flirt. Flirt like there was no tomorrow.

KELLY AND DYLAN FOREVER

Now that I've described the manscape of the *90210* set, I'm sure you want every sordid, sizzling detail of what really went on behind the scenes of *90210*, especially between Kelly and Dylan, meaning me and Luke.

Let's see: Where to begin?

One very hot, sunny day we were on location at the beach. We'd been shooting a scene out on the water, one that involved Jet Skis. Think of it as the *90210* version of us galloping bareback on horses down a deserted beach at sunset. You get the picture. I was wearing a PG-13, yet supercute bikini; Luke was wearing board shorts. And of course, just to make it hotter, we were both wearing big, bulky life jackets. Nineties sexy!

So, we were out there, buzzing around in the surf off Santa Monica. When the scene wrapped and we were breaking for lunch, I hopped on the back of a Jet Ski driven by a bodyguard while Luke took off on his own. I can't quite remember what happened next, but I think there was a fishing line cast off the pier, and the guy driving my Jet Ski didn't see it until it nearly sliced us both in two. Just before that could happen, he yelled, "Jump!" and so I did. Before I could catch my breath, it hit me. Or something hit me. Hard. I remember a loud thunk, and then under the water I went. I was out cold.

Next thing I knew, I was on the sand, a cluster of people around me. There was a paramedic on one side of me, gently placing a neck stabilizer around my shoulders, and another one, a cute one, leaning over me.

"What's your name?" he said.

I guess whatever I said came out all garbled. I wasn't quite awake yet, apparently.

So he asked another question: "Who is the current president?"

At that point, Luke chimed in: "Well, she wouldn't know the answer to that one even on the best of days."

"Fuck you, Luke!" I couldn't believe that was what came out of my mouth. But it did.

The cute paramedic called out, "She's all right, everybody."

But just to be safe, they whisked me off to the hospital, with Luke hovering nervously over me. Before I was even able to strip and get into one of those white gowns that showcases your bare ass, Luke blurted out, "I ran over you with the Jet Ski. I'm sorry."

You heard right, people: Luke Perry ran me over with a Jet Ski. Knocked me out cold while I was dog-paddling in the freezing-cold Pacific Ocean.

"Why did you jump in the water?" He was looking at me with his best Dylan McKay puppy-dog eyes. I hated when he did that.

I was too cold and too blurry-headed at that moment to tell him that I had leaped off that moving Jet Ski in order to save my life, but I did tell him later, and to this day, he still thinks that's a load of bullshit.

I had a wicked headache that night, and since then my memory hasn't been that great— Hold on just one dang minute. Luke Perry. Jet Ski. Shitty memory. It's all coming together. . . .

Actually, to be fair, I also sent Luke to the ER one time, too.

The product that we went through by the caseload on the set of *90210* was Binaca breath spray. Remember that stuff? It came in a little skinny palm-size aerosol can. With just one discreet spritz . . . your mouth was on fire!

We used it all the time, because in every episode there were at least one or two makeout sessions, and since we all lived on top of one another, using that stuff was the least we could do.

So one scorching afternoon, when it was about three hundred degrees out, Luke and I had a love scene to film on a makeshift soundstage out behind our ghetto studio in Van Nuys. We were all so hot and crabby, and Luke was poking at me, busting me about something, anything, just trying to get me to laugh, but what he was doing was really pissing me off. Just as they were setting up the shot, he mouthed off and . . .

Spritzzzzz! I shot him with my Binaca. And nailed him right in the eye.

It was an accident! I swear; it was an involuntary reaction to his badgering me, which, if you asked him, he'd tell you was one of his favorite things to do. He was having a ball, just pushing away at my buttons, and so I responded by pushing my own button. My hand just shot up, I pumped the Binaca, and Luke shut up. And so did his eye. Man, that thing proceeded to swell up to the size of a baseball (I am not kidding you), but instead of him being whisked off to the hospital the way I had been, he had to finish our scene.

I remember the camera guys kind of looked at him and cringed and then they turned his body so the blob that used to be his right eye was hidden from view. So I "made love" to the left side of his face, and even though it took some time, we got the shot and wrapped for the day.

Once the crew had broken down their equipment, they took Luke to the hospital, just to make sure he wasn't going to be permanently blinded. To this day he can still be such a baby about that incident, and I don't know why. It's not like it caused any permanent damage, like severe memory loss or anything! But despite how much pain we've caused each other, or maybe because of it, we're still friends.

I think our friendship was initially forged around what happened to us when the popularity of the show exploded. One time Luke and I had an appearance, just the two of us, at the San Diego Zoo. We weren't there five minutes when our appearance became the main attraction, and I think I can speak for both of us when I say that we actually did feel like we were on display like the animals. The fans who came out to see us grew into a huge and rowdy crowd pretty quickly. Our trip to the zoo had become a zoo. At this point in our careers, we just weren't very aware of our fame, because we spent all of our days sequestered on set out in happening Van Nuys. We were working all the time and had, very literally, been hidden away from the clamor and rigmarole surrounding *90210*, so we were pretty oblivious. Now here we were at the zoo, and Luke was all excited, because the promoters of the event had promised us a private tour of the animal exhibits after we'd signed a bunch of autographs. We were walked out onto a little makeshift platform, and before you know it, there were a hundred people, then five hundred, then a thousand, then two thousand. I am not exaggerating! The San Diego Zoo is enormous, and the crowd swelled so quickly that the promoters grabbed us both and led us through the animal enclosures to safety. There we were, running through the aviaries and the lion's run and past the elephant enclosure, and all Luke wanted to do was stop and look around—he wanted that private tour!

I don't know what it is about him, but he is one of my all-time favorite people, one of my best, most cherished friends. I can count on him for anything. Back in the day, that meant getting to sneak the odd puff off his cigarette, or swear like a truck driver because I didn't have to be all helpless and soft around him. I could just be myself. It was, and still is, like that for us.

He was the one man, besides my dad, who could see through my girlie-girl routine and call a spade a spade with me. He, better than anyone, knows that I'm no dumb blonde.

We see each other pretty regularly, and not too long ago I ran into him in the pediatrician's office where both of our kids are treated. I was so surprised to find him there that I kind of ran over toward him, my arms outstretched to hug him—and I promptly tripped over the scale and knocked my head on the wall. I don't know why, but he does that to me.

This is what I love about Luke: Even though he brings out the total dork in me, I know that he'll always have my back. If I were ever to fall, I'm certain he would catch me—unless, of course, he was the one who pushed me over the edge.

So there's the dirt on us. There's the big reveal about Kelly and Dylan. We are friends, and sometimes we had to make out at work. We are forever, Luke and I.

Actually all of us are: Ian, Brian, Jason, Gab, Tori, and Shannen. We are friends and family. Forever.

HOUSEKEEPING

I was nineteen when I bought my first house, a rickety little blue number on a hillside in Sherman Oaks. I experienced a lot of firsts there, including my first earthquake. I was in bed when it hit, which meant I was perched on a mattress that was on top of one of those flimsy metal frames that come with a new mattress. Well, that bed kind of bounced across the floor—with me in it. The first thing that went through my mind, after my brain registered "earthquake," was that AC/DC song, "You Shook Me All Night Long," and I remember looking around in fascination as art fell off the walls and things flew off of shelves and everything around me just rattled and rolled. It was wild. I have to say, there is something pretty theme-park-ride thrilling about your first California quake, especially when there is no serious damage that follows the ride.

I loved that little house, but sometimes I'd get a little spooked being there by myself, especially at night. It was built right on the street, which, when I first bought it, wasn't a problem at all, since I was just like every other teenager in LA, scrambling around behind the scenes trying to make something happen. But once *90210* started gaining that crazy momentum, I found my little house to be just a bit too exposed, and pretty much wide-open to any creep or stalker who wanted to walk right up to my windows and check me out. And yes, this did happen to me, but it was usually a carful of loud teenage girls—driven by one of their mothers—who was usually more excited than her kids to catch a glimpse of me.

I remember one night, though, when I could have sworn I heard someone lurking around the bushes outside, and so I called my neighbors, a lovely older couple who seemed supersolid and settled—and extremely safe. Well, the man, Don, came right over—with a giant shotgun draped over his arm. He looked around, gave me the all-clear, and then left. I was really glad he didn't have to use that gun.

At about this time, I was advised to get a housekeeper, because apparently this was what you did in Hollywood when you were a full-time working actress. I guessed it didn't matter that I didn't have much that needed cleaning, since I would come home from work and fill the time before going to bed cleaning or baking. But I kept hearing how having someone to help out at home would make my life easier, so I interviewed several people and ended up hiring a lovely young woman named Evangelina. She spoke next to no English and I spoke no Spanish, but somehow we figured out that she was going to work for me, and on her first day, she came, she cleaned, she conquered. I watched in awe as she moved around like a ninja, making my already tidy place spotless. When she was finished, I paid her and thanked her profusely—in English, while she nodded and thanked me in Spanish. We both stood there, nodding and thanking each other, and we did this for as long as we could until it just got really quiet. Evangelina wasn't leaving, and I didn't understand why. Finally, after standing there staring at each other for about five minutes, she said, "Okay. I be back." Then she turned and walked out the door.

Sure enough, the next week, on the same day, at the same time, she came back. When I got home that day, I noticed that she'd subtly arranged things so that it felt more like someone actually lived there, as opposed to being the crash pad of a lonely teenage girl who was off working fifteen hours a day. When I walked through the door, I was struck by how thrilled I was to see her radiant smile, and I realized that I was feeling kind of sad about saying good-bye to her. Again, we thanked each other. Again, we stood there, by my front door, in awkward silence. Then she nodded, smiled, and said, "Okay. I be back."

This little routine of ours went on for a few months, but after each one of her visits, I began to feel that my house was being infused with her warm, loving essence, and I finally caught on that Evangelina was beginning to transform my tiny, largely uninhabited house into a home. If I brought in something new—say, some throw pillows, or a new duvet cover, or a vase—she'd exclaim about how lovely it was (she was a huge, early fan of my decorating sensibilities). She'd ask about my work, in her halting English, while she fussed over something, and I realized that, with my mom back in Arizona a lot of the time, it felt wonderful to have someone else looking out for me in a warm, maternal way. Evangelina, who is only about ten years older than me, has the most giant and generous heart of all time. And today, she's got a beautiful grown daughter to prove it. Soon her once-a-week visits became twice-a-week visits, and before I knew it, Evangelina was an essential part of my heart team. We've been together ever since.

Now I had two friends in LA—Patrice and Evangelina, two women I knew I could count on—and I began to think that maybe I would be able to make it; maybe I would be able to hack it here in Tinsletown on my own. If I had had a beret back then, maybe I would have even tossed it in the air, à la Mary Tyler Moore.

For the first time in a very, very long time, maybe the first time ever, really, I felt like I was beginning to put down some roots.

I LIKE YOUR STYLE

My life really did go from zero to sixty when *90210* broke out, and so did my visibility—and viability—as an actress. When I think back on it now, it's pretty insane that I went from being a high school junior in Arizona to being an established television actress in Hollywood in just three very short years. It was a change that wasn't just fast as hell; it was confusing and difficult to make sense of, because on the outside I seemed to have it all: financial security, a great job, a sweet new boyfriend (more on that later), and a great family (though they were all too far away). But going from being a sheltered, lonely, and shy teenager to a very public figure in such a short amount of time didn't quite jell inside. I mean, honestly? It still seems really strange to me. I still see myself as a girl from a tiny dot of a place in the middle of no-where, at times, and so I'm always trying to get the inner reality of who I am to match up with what the outer world sees. I'm not complaining, of course, just saying it's a bit of a paradox. And often a challenge.

Lucky for me, I've met some really great people who have helped me stay grounded and real, no matter what the media says about who I am or what is made about whatever happens to be going on in my life. The person who has probably been the closest to me since I was launched out of deep, deep obscurity is my friend Adele, a remarkable woman and partner in crime whom I've now known for half my life.

I met Adele right around the time I bought my second home. I had just turned twenty, and when security really did start to become an issue, I sold my sweet, tiny first house and moved into a place that had the kind of security being a recognizable star requires. It was a great house, set back on a pretty sizable piece of property and down a very long driveway that was hidden behind a giant wrought-iron gate. The house was big and it needed a lot of work, and so Mr. Showbiz convinced me that, if I were really going to undertake the renovation I envisioned, I'd need more than just Evangelina's help: I'd need a personal assistant.

I honestly didn't quite know what this meant, and I still had trouble asking Evangelina to do things like, say, empty the dishwasher: I mean, I had two hands, right? I wasn't helpless, and I hated burdening people. Even by then, I'd pretty much mastered that kind of do-it-yourselfness that can, if you're not careful, actually be mistaken for the kind of independence that others interpret as your not needing them, and then you'll find yourself more alone than is good for you, but hey . . . I'm digressing into thoughts that are way too deep here, so back to the story at hand. In my mind, I pictured a personal assistant as someone wearing a serious suit and intimidating eyewear and a severe updo who would be chasing me—a girl who pretty much did nothing but work—with a day planner and a pencil and a disapproving smirk on her face. What on earth would I do with a person like that? Clearly nothing, because that is not what the universe had in mind for me when it came to hiring a personal assistant.

Enter Adele.

Mr. Showbiz had put an ad in *Variety* that read, "High-profile actress seeks assistant." Then he met with a bunch of people and winnowed it down to the top three or four. Then he set up brief meetings for me with each of them. Mind you, these were all very well-qualified and decent people; now I just had to choose one. Well, the first interview was just plain embarrassing—at least for me. I mean, I sat in front of a woman who was probably twenty years older than me, and I clutched her résumé in my hand while she regaled me with stories of how she'd whipped some Hollywood heavy hitters' lives into shape. I was impressed—and terrified by her. Next, I met someone who was nice, but when I couldn't remember her name, I knew she wasn't the one.

Then I met Adele, a woman only a year or so older than me who had, to my completely uncool mind, the absolute greatest sense of style. In she came, wearing black combat boots, cropped and cuffed black pin-striped suit pants, and a white puffy blouse (very circa 1994), and I thought, *Wow. This girl could definitely help me in the fashion department.* It's important to note that while I was wearing a long denim shirt, a white T-shirt, and a gold cross around my neck, I too, wore . . . combat boots. Even though mine were brown suede, there it was: the essential mind-meld, the sign that we were meant to be together, because we both had on chunky boots. Adele had worked in Hollywood before, as a personal assistant to an actress, even, but she had been in New York for a few years, and she was only now getting back to LA. There was something so not Hollywood about her. Something so down-to-earth. I got a sense that she'd be good for me, on top of being a good assistant. I hired her on the spot. And it was, I have to say, one of the best decisions I have ever made.

Adele became pretty indispensable immediately, because I dived headfirst right into renovating that house. This was no minor tweaking of the decor, mind you; this was a full gut renovation, and I had a great contractor named John, but needed someone to be on-site, acting as my eyes and ears while I was out in Van Nuys at work. Adele took this all on without flinching, and so immediately, her positive influence on my life was evident.

Working with Adele and John the contractor, I learned pretty quickly that gutting a house and putting it back together turned out to be the kind of large-scale project I could really sink my teeth into. I dug it! I found demolition of any kind to be a blast, and doing all the work of consulting with architects and poring over plans and making decisions about where, say, a wall ought to go, kind of . . . relaxes me. Since that first redo (on what Adele affectionately refers to as the Woodstock house), I've renovated three or four more houses, and I've come to realize that, deep down, I'm really a frustrated interior designer who is most at home around tile guys, plumbers, and other nuts-and-bolts home-building pros. I'm definitely more comfortable in a torn-down house than I am on the red carpet, and if I had to identify one superhero strength I might have, I'd say it's renovating houses.

I changed everything about that place on Woodstock, including putting in a rose garden—I got to buy a farm-grade tiller!—and adding a huge freestanding guesthouse in the large, parklike backyard.

Adele became my partner in crime in so many ways, so quickly. She had an office in my house, and it became Jennie Command Central. Every morning we'd meet there and go over what had to be done; then we'd start talking about stuff we just wanted to do. We were both superprofessional and hardworking, but if we found ourselves in the Woodstock house together with some time on our hands, we'd get really crafty together: We did a lot of baking, or we'd garden. At one point we really got into jewelry making, and it kind of got out of control: We made bracelets and earrings, and it was such a crazy obsession that we made all of our Christmas gifts. I also agreed to do a *90210*

Christmas special—but only if my friend Adele could be in it, too. So the camera crews came to my house and filmed us while Adele and I made cutout cookies.

Adele also served as my security detail. Well, my security blanket, anyway. She figured out that she could coax me out to the mall if we went at ten a.m. on a weekday, because that's when all the crazed *90210* fans would be in school. Or she'd come out to the set in Van Nuys to hang out and I'd find myself relaxing and laughing and having fun during the times I'd normally just go off to rest and be by myself. She was also an excellent pet wrangler (at one point, I had seventeen animals, which meant Adele spent a lot of time at the vet, too). Plus, she could make me laugh harder than anybody, or she could just be by my side without either of us feeling the need to talk at all. I liked that about her. A lot.

Most significantly, Adele helped me come out of my shell, in terms of getting to know other people. She was so open and forthcoming that she taught me, by example, how to engage with others, even if where they were coming from was a place I had no clue about. The best example of this happened when we had been working together for about two weeks. I can't remember where we were going, but we were in my car and as we were driving down the freeway, Adele said, 'We've been with each other all day every day for a while now, and I thought it would be good to share some things about myself with you." I was driving when she said this, and she just plowed ahead: "I'm in a relationship with a woman, who is also an actress, and we've been together for about four years. We've recently been discussing the possibility of ending our relationship, and I thought you ought to know that I may be moving in the next few months and that, though this is a painful and difficult time, I will work hard and will be very professional." I was so blown away by Adele's maturity and candor, and I realize now that she sounded very much like the excellent psychotherapist she is today.

Adele is one of those people whom other people want to know. She's warm but not intrusive, wise but not bossy. She's the best listener I've ever met. Adele was, and is, all about the truth: she wanted to know how I was feeling, what I was thinking—she has this gift of cutting through all the BS with anyone she's fond of. I credit her with being real with me in a way that helped me to relax and just be myself with her, which is something I needed at that time in my life: the friend who tells it like it is. Telling the truth, though not easy when you struggle to be honest with yourself, is always the right, liberating thing to do, and Adele, more than anyone, has helped me realize this.

Talk about capable. That's Adele in a nutshell. Within weeks of coming to work with me, she was not only overseeing the renovation of my house, but she also planned my first wedding. But more on that later. First I want to share with you one of the crazier episodes of my life with Adele.

DON'T OPEN THAT DOOR

Kombucha.

I'm betting you've heard of this crazy stuff, which is considered to be one of the magical, age-defying, disease-busting elixirs of life that you can find bottled up and on refrigerator shelves at bodegas and grocery stores across the land. Never mind that it will set you back about five bucks a bottle. This stuff may promote health, but it tastes gross, and the growing of it is even grosser.

How do I know this, you ask?

Because I used to grow the stuff—way back before it was cool, before it was ever, probably, legal. And I didn't just grow it: I traveled with it. But I get ahead of myself.

It was circa 1994 and I was well settled into the routine of *90210* when I heard about this "magic" (not that kind) mushroom that, when fermented, created a tea that would impart all kinds of health benefits, not the least of which was an overall sense of well-being and serenity, which I desperately needed.

Enter the kombucha mushroom, which is no mushroom at all—oh, no. It's a gooey blob of yeasts glommed onto bacteria, and when it's left to sit in a brew of black tea and sugar . . . strange and mystical things happen. The "mushroom" (a gross, quivering, jellylike disk) blooms and ferments, and if you take good care of it, it will throw off a spawn (baby kombucha!) in about ten days. At that point (once it's multiplied) you drink the black tea that it's been sitting in. Delicious! And then you begin the process all over again.

Here's the thing, though: To grow kombucha you have to put it in a warm, dark place and not disturb it. And by not disturb it, I mean it needs to never see the light of day, and no playing of Pearl Jam at high volumes within twenty miles of the thing.

So I had kombucha mushrooms floating in black tea soup, covered with cheesecloth, hidden in the closets throughout my home. Anyone who came to my place knew something was up, because my house smelled like the inside of a giant, unwashed pickle barrel. It smelled just the way kombucha tastes—only about five thousand times stronger. Every week or so, I'd open a closet, find that the mushroom had given birth, and then I'd strain off the disgusting tea it made and drink it.

Yup. I did that.

But it wasn't just me.

Adele, my faithful friend, was my kombucha partner in crime.

I remember during one *90210* hiatus when I headed off to Toronto to make a TV movie, and somehow or another, we managed to smuggle a new spawn into the ritzy hotel where we'd be living. We would be on location for about three weeks, which was just enough time for the kombucha magic cycle to happen a couple of times. If we could get our little mushroom in, we'd be able to guzzle the gnarly fermented "tea" a few times, certain that if we did, we'd both live to be at least one hundred and seventy-five.

But here's the thing. You've got to treat the kombucha like it's a colicky baby that's been up all night and seriously needs to catch up on its rest. This means you put it in a glass container, cover it with something that will keep it clean but yet will allow air to pass through it, and then you put it in a cool, dark place where it will be undisturbed. Easy.

Whenever there was kombucha in the house, Adele and I would talk as though we were professional golf commentators, in these low, soft, supercalm voices, and we would tiptoe around, barefoot. It was crucial that we not disturb the kombucha, because we knew how crazy-sensitive that stuff was; one slipup and we might wind up with a toxic blob that would grow out of control and would consume whatever was in its way. Then we'd really be in trouble.

Actually, I had read somewhere that kombucha, a living, stinky thing, had, some believed, the intelligence of a dolphin. I don't know if I would go that far, but I certainly had a deep respect for the kombucha. A certain naive reverence, if you will. I wanted this stuff to cure what ailed me, and so I ascribed all kinds of super healing powers to the stuff, and my hopeful attitude helped in more ways than one, given how nasty that stuff tasted.

But back to our hotel room in Toronto. We were all settled in, but we had a bit of a dilemma. How would we keep the housekeeping staff from disturbing our kombucha distillery? Adele came up with the brilliant idea to make a straightforward sign that read: Do Not Open This Door Under Any Circumstances! She wrote this out in giant, black block letters and taped it to the closet door. Clearly anyone who came into our suite would know that something was up, because our clothes and shoes were all over the place, stuffed into the dressers and hanging on the backs of doors and along the curtain rod that hung over the bathtub. There was something that was not clothes or a suitcase in that closet—but what?

I mean, that sign had to be pretty enticing, right?

Certainly, if I were a housekeeper and I came into a room with a sign like that, I'd be pretty tempted to at least sneak a peek.

That is, of course, if I could stand the kombucha stench, which got stronger with each passing day. At this stage of my own personal kombucha phase, I was pretty used to it, but even Adele and I would flinch when we'd open the door after eight or so hours away from the room. Once we could breathe again, we'd look at each other, smile knowingly, and say, "Ah. Kombucha!" in those crazy golf voices we would automatically slip into.

I don't know if anyone at that hotel ever broke the kombucha code and opened that door, but I do know that no one stole our mushroom and we were able to not only enjoy a few rounds of kombucha tea, but lo and behold, our mushroom gave birth on location! It was customary to give the babies away to others (kombucha culture was all about sharing the health and the wealth), but I don't recall whether we left it for our housekeeper or not.

Come to think of it, I don't know whether we ever took that sign down, so . . . even though it's been twenty years . . . perhaps our kombucha mushroom is still there, in that hotel closet in Toronto, multiplying and multiplying and . . .

I shudder to think. . . . And now I'm thirsty, too.

RUNNING DOWN THE AISLE

By the time I met Adele, I'd been seeing a guy named Dan for a while. Dan was an aspiring musician I met through another musician friend of mine. He was tall, big, cute. And he reminded me a lot of my dad in some ways, the dad that I remembered from my childhood: the big, strong, charismatic, totally lovable blond. Once my mom had moved back to Arizona, Dan moved in and I converted the guesthouse into a fully equipped music studio for him, complete with a sound booth and very expensive soundboards and all the state-of-the-art recording equipment that we could possibly cram in there. So while I logged my long days on the *90210* set in Van Nuys, Dan, a drummer, immersed himself in the music scene.

We were two kids playing house, taking my crazy "fame" ride together. Now I didn't have to walk the red carpet alone; Dan would be there for me. And now, when I had to do publicity or promotional events, I had someone to hold my hand when things felt overwhelming or my sense of vulnerability would start to tip over into panic. Most important, I had someone there when I came home at night. This was incredibly reassuring, and it gave my life the kind of settled vibe that I had been aching for.

Dan was a nice, nice guy with a big heart, and so the people around me accepted him (at least, most of them did, anyway), and even my family, who put him through the "So what, exactly, do you want from our daughter/sister?" paces, grew to like him, too, I think.

When I look back at the twenty-year-old me now, I realize that so much of the anxiety I felt wasn't about the sudden fame or the crazy fans, though all of that was pretty stressful for sure, even when I learned to dodge most of that stress by working my butt off on set for more than half of every day, or by burying myself in a big-ass home-remodeling project. No, the biggest source of stress in my life was my near-crippling fear that I'd lose my dad. By then, he'd suffered several more heart attacks and had undergone more surgeries, and his poor body was just beaten up and falling apart. It was clear to us all, including my dad, that he was never going to get better, that his health was on a pretty precarious slope, and that there was no chance of things reversing course. It was really just a question of how many blows his poor old heart could take before the jig was up. My dad, poor guy, was saddled with a ticking time bomb of a heart, and I was always holding my breath, waiting for that awful, dreaded phone call to come.

I was afraid that if I lost him, I would lose all sense of who I was and where I'd come from. And my fears, as it turns out, weren't unfounded: Once, when my dad was visiting me and Dan, he had a heart attack right there in front of me. The ambulance came, we whisked him to the hospital, and he was immediately admitted into the ICU. However traumatizing this event was for me, it turned out to be a great stroke of luck for my dad, because he'd been so sick and hospitalized so many times in Arizona that his insurance was pretty much maxed out there, but in California he was covered. Phew! Another bullet dodged.

I was so grateful I had Dan to lean on when all of this was happening, and so it doesn't surprise the forty-one-year-old me that, even though I was so young, I pretty much ran down the aisle with him as soon as I could, marrying him just two weeks after my twenty-second birthday. I can see now that my reasons for that first marriage weren't very mature, and certainly there were people around me who gently tried to persuade me that maybe this wasn't the best way to go. Luke, for instance. He liked Dan—I mean, there wasn't much not to like—but he just didn't see him as husband material. He didn't come to the wedding, but he did give us a gift: a Mister Loaf bread maker, and the message in this wasn't lost on me. And later, Mr. Showbiz told me that before the ceremony started, Aaron Spelling turned to him and said, "When they ask if anyone objects, who is going to speak up? You or me?" I couldn't see or say this clearly back then, but the truth was, marrying Dan, sad to say, wasn't about Dan. It was about looking for security. It was about wanting to feel looked after. So when Dan asked me to marry him, I said yes.

Adele, who'd been with me only a very short time, took over and planned the whole thing. With a ten-thousand-dollar budget, she put together the most beautiful, sweet wedding, to which we invited only a handful of our nearest and dearest. The writer Marianne Williamson married us, and the whole thing was pulled off in complete secrecy. It was private and quiet and beautiful. Because of how crazy things had become around the show, we had our wedding in my friend Damon's mom's backyard (Damon had introduced me and Dan) in Beverly Hills, away from the prying eyes of the paparazzi. I remember it was a gorgeous, clear Southern California day, and my dad was there to walk me down the aisle, just as I'd hoped. We were happy, Dan and I, at least for those first few months, when being newlyweds was so novel and fun. But once the energy and adrenaline of all that wedding planning wore off, and it was just the two of us again, it hit me pretty quickly that I had no business being married, that I was still, despite what my life looked like, extremely young and unworldly and not at all prepared to be someone's wife. Plus, I was working crazy long days, and Dan was out doing the musician thing at night. What were we doing being married? We never saw each other, for God's sake. I think I was a pretty excellent girlfriend, and the last thing I wanted to do was to hurt Dan, but in the end, I knew deep down that we just didn't have enough in common to build a future on. I wasn't happy. Was Dan? I honestly didn't even know, because he was busy doing his thing, while I did mine. Maybe, I was starting to think, running down the aisle wasn't the best thing to have done . . . but you know what? Now, looking back, I'd say it was. I had the classic "starter" marriage, and anyone who has had one of these knows that they're excellent labs for learning exactly what you don't want your married life to look like. It was a pretty invaluable lesson, and because of that, it's a decision I don't regret for a second. But that doesn't mean it didn't cause me some serious agony.

I'd be on the phone with Adele late at night, crying and so stressed out about my failing marriage, and she'd talk me down and tell me that I'd get a handle on it. So while all of this confusion about my marriage was going on, I made another big family decision that I needed to have my mom and dad closer. So I bought a ranch in one of the incredibly beautiful rural valleys a couple of hours north of Los Angeles, and I persuaded my parents to pack everything up—including all the animals—and come to California.

Now I owned not one, but two properties in California, which meant, I guess, that I was putting down some roots and staking a pretty serious claim here.

With my parents nearer, I was hoping that I would finally be able to stitch my family back together again. I was figuring it out. Slowly but surely, little by little.

But I still had to figure out what to do about Dan. There was a work hiatus coming up and I would be executive producing and starring in a made-for-TV movie called *An Unfinished Affair*. I'd be heading off to Arizona for a month, and this would give me the time away I needed to sort things out.

At least, that was what I thought.

THE REAL DEAL

When you're an executive producer, you're involved in all aspects of putting a project together, and so one of the tasks I had to take on for *An Unfinished Affair* was helping to select the cast. There was a part for an actor about my age, who would play one of my love interests in the movie. (In fact, he'd play the *son* of my primary love interest. . . . I know, right? How could I not seize the opportunity to play a true bad girl, after more than five years of clicking my heels together on *90210*?) I sat down with Mr. Showbiz, who was my co–executive producer on this project, and together we watched a handful of audition tapes and there he was: Peter Facinelli, a young actor out of New York. He was perfect for the part, so we hired him.

So off I went to Arizona, with Adele and a huge need to both clear my head and immerse myself in work.

Heady, heady stuff.

But guess what. Sometimes, when you're all about minding your business, you can leave a little back door to your heart unattended, and sometimes, when this happens and you're not looking, the wildest, most unexpectedly wonderful things can happen.

When I stepped onto that movie set and met Peter . . . *kaboom!* It was like getting flattened by a meteor. I had never felt so bowled over in the presence of a guy before. Never.

Thank God Adele was with me, because before I could lose my head completely, I had to address the situation with Dan. I had been thinking we needed to separate for some time, but I kept pushing it off, always finding an excuse and telling myself I would deal with it soon. Well, apparently, soon was now. I remember Adele handing me this giant, awkward cell phone (remember those things? they looked like you were holding a brick up to your ear) and standing there, holding my hand, as I made that incredibly grown-up call.

Dan couldn't have been more gracious and understanding—and in full agreement. With that one call, I had ended my marriage, and I spent the rest of that month bonding with my new costar, my new best friend, my new love. Oh, my God—we had a blast.

When I was in LA, working five days a week on *90210*, it was all about business. I used my hiatus time to branch out and do other projects. These jobs were always on location, and these little monthlong shoots sometimes served as a way for me to let my hair down. And Adele would come along and we'd just get silly, and . . . a little wild. I mean, remember, people, this was 1995. I was twenty-three! We'd hang out with the cast and crew of the movie, drink a little more than we would back home; then we'd go out and listen to live music. There might be a game or two of strip poker, a few late-night skinny dips in the hotel pool—that kind of thing.

Peter and I couldn't have been more different, at least on the face of things. He was first-generation American, having grown up in a big Italian family in Queens, New York. He was the youngest of four, the only boy, and he was the apple of everyone's eye (including, pretty much right away, mine). He was so adventurous and playful, a city kid through and through. He was young and a perfect mix of cool and dorky, and so open and alive.

We were like two peas in a pod, two kids in a candy shop. We just wanted to play and explore and get to know everything we possibly could about each other. With Peter, I felt like I was discovering that the world was, indeed, big, fat, and round, but more than that, I was discovering that you could feel terrified and wonderful, all at the same time. This was big, big, happy news to me, given how anxious I'd been for so much of my life.

Now I felt kind of like an astronaut in outer space: still safely tethered to the mother ship, yet way, way out there, floating free among the stars. It was the best feeling in the world.

He was adorable. Handsome. Gorgeous. God, we were young when we met: I was twenty-three and Peter was twenty-one. Man, when I look back on it now . . . I mean, we were so freakin' young! And even though I'd been married before, I had never felt this way about a guy.

Our love affair was so passionate, so sweet, so wonderful. Peter moved out to Los Angeles pretty immediately. He rented an apartment in West Hollywood but we spent all of our time together. It was such a blast being with him: We'd found each other and we were finding ourselves.

It was the most beautiful, exciting time of my life.

BEAUTIFUL LIGHT

You know how one day you can just wake up and before you know it your whole life has taken a crazy, fantastic, unexpected turn? How all of a sudden, you find yourself going down a road you never even imagined, a road that leads you to the most beautiful, soulful, meaningful stuff possible?

Well, that happened to me when I was twenty-four. I was fully immersed in my career and felt like I was finally doing a better job of riding the fame wave. I'd just recently fallen completely head over heels in love with a really great guy. I think we'd been seeing each other for about six months or so when we found out I was pregnant. I was stunned. He was stunned. But as soon as we got over the initial shock of it, we were a hundred percent thrilled and excited about it. It definitely felt like one of those moments when the universe taps you on the shoulder and says, "Look: I've got this incredible gift for you." And luckily, we both knew that and were grateful for it. Besides, we were just so madly in love. It just made all that sweeter.

My parents were supportive, too, and Peter's family, to their credit, also embraced me and our news with gusto and great love.

Now I just had to figure out how to tell Mr. Spelling our happy news, which you'd think wouldn't be that big a deal, since I'd been working for him for about seven years at that point.

But right around the time that I found out I was pregnant, another actress, a woman named Hunter Tylo, was embroiled in a huge, messy lawsuit with Aaron and the producers of the show she'd been on—a show she'd promptly been fired from when she told them she was pregnant. I think she'd just been awarded the whopping sum of $4.8 million (the jury had actually doubled what she had been seeking in damages), and so I felt pretty certain that I wouldn't lose my job, but still . . . it was an awkward time to be bringing up the "p"-word with this particular group of executives.

Besides, what are you supposed to do when you play a high school girl who wears superfashionable (i.e.: slightly slutty) clothes and you find yourself staring down the prospect of packing on fifty or sixty pounds over the course of a few short months, while the cameras are still rolling?

First, I had to tell the big boss, and if I'm remembering this correctly, I actually called him myself. Aaron couldn't have been more gracious, more supportive of me, and he assured me that he'd take care of breaking the news to the whole company, which he did in a way that was completely awesome and wonderful, because everybody—and I mean everybody—was excited about the big news (or else).

We were in the midst of filming our sixth or seventh season at that point, and I think Kelly and Brandon were paired up at that time in the story line, but rather than try to figure out how to write the pregnancy into the script, the powers that be decided to conceal it completely from our young, impressionable audience, and of course, this was totally fine with me. I didn't want to become the prime-time poster girl for an underage character getting knocked up.

The first few months were no big deal, in terms of hiding the pregnancy, but after that first trimester, everything started to pop: my belly, my boobs, my nose, my feet, my hands. My wardrobe fittings were never a picnic to begin with—think of a weird form of torture where you're asked to hold your arms straight out from your body for inexplicably long stretches of time, while fabric is tucked and pinned and pinched around you. I don't know what it is, but costume fittings give me the worst backaches of all time. But as I started to swell up, they became superchallenging. The costumers would do this crazy kind of origami where they'd swathe me in a ton of fabric, then pin and tuck it so that the top part looked kind of stylish, while below my bust there was usually just so much fabric that you couldn't even tell I had a body, never mind one that was packing on the pounds and inches at an alarming rate. Once I was in costume, I'd be shot from the waist up, or holding a giant shopping bag, or, say, sitting on a couch with a pillow in my lap. The camera crew became really skilled at hiding my growing bump.

Then, at around the month-six mark, my bump became a mountain. I started to feel like the Stay Puft Marshmallow Man from *Ghostbusters*, staggering and lumbering around the set, trying to look all cute and seductive but just superaware that I always had to pee and that I might explode all over my castmates at any given moment.

I did not feel like a hot young thing. I felt like a hot, giant mess.

Toward the very end of my pregnancy, when I was about eight and a half months along, we were filming our final episode of the season and Jason was directing. The story line revolved around some Beverly High event, like a prom or homecoming, and so I had to wear a tentlike gown that was strategically folded and pinned to hide what Jason began to affectionately refer to as Bob. At that point we knew that I was pregnant with a girl, but that didn't matter to Jason. My bump—I mean my Mount Everest—became almost like another character during filming that week, and Jason would confer with the camerapeople about how to handle Bob in this or that scene in a way that was pretty funny, and pretty sweet. I spent most of that "dance" or whatever it was standing behind a high table, acting all chipper and girlie and teenagery, while my back ached and my feet swelled. I had just turned twenty-five, but here I was, pretending to still be in high school. When they finally called it a wrap, I was so relieved. I swear I could hear all those pins and clips that held all that fabric together on me pop and give.

With that we were finished for the season, and we would be heading into a short hiatus, which, clearly, was a huge blessing for me. I badly needed to prop my puffy ankles up and take care of a few things . . . like buying diapers and getting a crib set up. I'd been so busy at work that I hadn't done any nesting, and so we had to scramble to prepare for the blessed event.

Once I found out I was pregnant, I sold the Woodstock house and Peter and I rented a really secluded house up off of Mulholland Drive. The house was down a narrow little driveway that led through a dark, slightly foreboding jungle of trees. This house was so remote, so tucked away on a really lushly landscaped lot, that you really did forget the rest of the world when you were up there. I loved this.

When my break finally came, Peter was off on location, making an independent film somewhere in Texas, so my mom and dad moved into the small guesthouse on the property to be there for me while Peter was away.

My mom dived right into those nesting chores with me, helping me to wash teeny-tiny clothes and little blankets, and when it came time to set up the nursery, she gasped when she opened the door to the baby's room to find that nothing had been set up. The only thing in the room was a giant pile of unopened boxes stacked up in the middle of the room. With my mom taking the lead, we tore through all of that stuff and set that room up in no time, complete with homemade curtains, which was a good thing, because it wasn't too long after that, maybe only a day or so, that I went into labor.

One night, sometime in those really quiet early hours of the morning, I woke up and felt a strange twinge. Then I felt another one. And another one. So I called over to the guesthouse and told my mom that I thought I might be going into labor. She and my dad immediately got up and came to get me. I remember my dad was just so excited, like a little kid at Christmas. While my mom drove and I rode in the passenger seat, my dad, who was riding in the backseat, was all squished up between the seats, his head poking out between me and my mom, and he was backseat driving like mad as we made our way through those dark, still canyons and down into the city, to Cedars-Sinai Medical Center in Los Angeles.

The job of tracking Peter down fell to my GBF (gay best friend), Bryan, and he was able to reach Peter and get him on a flight out of Texas, but then Peter got stuck in Phoenix for a layover. He called me from a pay phone there and labored right along with me, saying all sorts of encouraging birthing things to me, while my mother held a giant, primitive cell phone up to my ear.

God, I was so happy to have him on the phone with me, but I have to say (and I know you ladies who've been there know what I'm talking about), every time he'd say something encouraging, like, "You can do it!" or, "Breathe!" I wanted to take that giant cell phone and throw it across the room.

In other words, it sucks to be on the phone when you're a sweaty, heaving mess who is ten centimeters dilated and so far gone into the la-la land of end-stage labor that you're pretty certain your head is going to spin 360 degrees and you are going to start speaking in tongues and levitate off the bed.

When I was no longer able to speak, my mother continued to hold the phone up to my ear so I could hear Peter and so, presumably, he could hear every grunt and scream and wail coming out of me. And then I gritted my teeth, turned all my energies inward, and it happened: I pushed and she came and . . . that was when the phone died.

Just before it did, though, Peter got to hear our darling baby cry and he knew she was here and safe. About an hour later, he came bursting through the door with roses and a teddy bear in hand, a look of utter joy and wonderment on his young, perfect face.

When I think of that moment now, with him holding our sweet, delicate little baby in his arms for the first time, it can still nearly bring me to my knees. It was such a profoundly beautiful moment in our lives. She was here! We named our sweet daughter Luca Bella, which means "beautiful light" in Italian. She was so perfect and so luminous, our shiny little star. We were both madly in love with her and even more madly in love with each other. My life, it seemed, just couldn't get any better.

THE CUTEST GIRL ON SET

Peter and I brought our Luca Bella home and we immediately slipped into the wonderfully out-of-it paradise of new parenthood. We were all about cooing and cuddling and sleeping. And eating and soothing and sleeping. It was a very sweet, quietly blissed-out time for us, but in the end, like all the best things in life, it was just too short.

Duty—meaning my *90210* contract—called. The summer hiatus was nothing more than a quick month off, and even though I'd almost literally just given birth, I had no choice but to go back to work.

We quickly ran through our child-care options, which included hiring a full-time nanny to come in and virtually live with us, and enlisting my mom (and dad) to stay nearby and help out around Peter's work schedule. Or . . . I could bring baby Luca to work with me.

We were still in that early, intensive bonding phase, Luca and I, and I just couldn't imagine parting with her—even if it meant having to bring her out to Van Nuys to that grubby, run-down soundstage that had been my home away from home for more than six years by then. I discussed this with Peter and the rest of my inner circle and we all agreed that I ought to give it a try, and if it didn't work out, well, then we'd figure something out and adjust.

So when our work hiatus ended, there went my maternity leave, too. On the dreaded first day I was due back to work, I dragged myself up and out of bed before the sun came up, swaddled up my teeny-tiny newborn, and gently buckled her into the car seat in my SUV. Then, in the dark, quiet hours of earliest morning, I drove us both to work.

It was pretty jarring bringing a newborn baby into our intensely industrious, high-energy work lair. It was like bringing a baby, say, into a strip club: She was just so out of place in that environment. I might as well have brought a tiger cub with me—the soundstage where we worked was barely fit for adults, never mind children. Everyone was so excited to meet her, of course, and there was a lot of oohing and ahhing and hugging—for about thirty seconds. Then it got awkward, because we were on the clock, so everyone started bustling around, Luca got hungry, and I had to put on my game face and act like this was just another day at the office. But, man, let me tell you: It's a challenge pretending you're an angsty teenager when in reality you're a new mom with squishy boobs and a radically altered body whose head and hormones are still spinning wildly.

I do need to clarify, though, that I didn't just show up with Luca in my arms unannounced: A tremendous amount of planning and preparation had to go into my returning to work with a child in tow, and I have to give Mr. Showbiz endless credit for how artfully he helped arrange this. He had to really work his magic, and his butt off, to negotiate with the producers so that we could create some kind of safe, serene, and secure environment for me and my baby. The soundstage was, as noted, a grimy hole of a place, a big drafty warehouselike building that was purposely unadorned and uninsulated, a place that could withstand the rapid building and dismantling of sets, a place that was user-friendly to hammer-wielding union contractors but definitely not babies.

The solution we came up with was this: I bought a fully loaded RV that would be parked on the lot. This would be my new dressing room, Luca's home away from home, and her day-care facility all rolled into one. Not only would the RV be stocked with diapers, a crib, and age-appropriate toys, but I would need to hire a nanny to be a part of this rolling baby show, someone whom I could trust to be with Luca when I was needed on set. During the ramping up of this very personal "Take Your Kid to Work" campaign, I was given the number of a professional nanny service, an outfit with an impeccable reputation, and which many an actress had used and raved about. I went through the interview process and hired a lovely woman who was about twenty years older than me. I learned, shortly after I hired her, that she'd also recently given birth to a child, and it pretty much broke my heart to think that someone else was somewhere looking after her child while here she was, looking after mine. I don't know if she was pouring all of her own thwarted maternal love into caring for my Luca, but every time I left the set and came back to the RV, my heart would jump a little when I'd catch sight of this lovely woman, who was a stranger to me, fawning over my daughter. I don't know if the uncomfortable feeling this gave me was raw jealousy or if it was some kind of maternal bell that, I would learn with experience, rang whenever I sensed that something wasn't quite right. Whatever it was, I couldn't shake it, and so I made the decision that I had to have someone I already knew, someone who was virtually family to me, look after Luca. So with as much grace as I could muster, I let the agency nanny go and I brought in my Evangelina to work alongside me out in Van Nuys as Luca's nanny. Now, instead of being my housekeeper, Evangelina's task would be to take exquisitely good care of Luca—just the way she had always taken care of me.

With Evangelina in place, Team Luca was complete. Now I could get back to work with some peace of mind.

And what a relief! Evangelina proved to be more than up to the challenge, and she finished out the run of *90210* with us. As soon as Luca could talk, she christened Evangelina "Nina," and that's when she became our Nina for good. Since then, she's helped raise all three of our girls and . . . she's still with us! Nina is absolutely part of our innermost circle, a cherished family member, an incredibly loving, stable, and constant force for good in all of our lives.

Even with Nina there, getting back into sync with Kelly Taylor and leaving my real life and family behind was a challenge at first, but I was able to do it and to pull it off for the next three years.

ZEN AND THE MAKEUP CHAIR

I t's amazing how your perspective on things can change so radically once you've had a baby. Not that long before Luca was born, sitting in a makeup chair had been a certain kind of torture for me, so much so that I even once took the drastic step of having all of my hair chopped off because I just couldn't stand sitting for the amount of time it took to do a blowout. I just could not do it. One. More. Time.

Now, sleep deprived and cranky, with huge, achy milk boobs weighing me down, I found the prospect of spending two hours in a makeup chair to be right up there with a first-class vacation on a deserted tropical island.

By the time I staggered into the makeup room and backed myself into the waiting chair, the joint was usually jumping—and this was at six a.m. Music would be blaring, the air would be filled with cigarette smoke, people would be laughing and regaling whoever would listen with stories about their latest acts of debauchery, and once the blow-dryers started up, the din in the place would rise to a crazy, catty pitch.

That was when I'd sink into a beautifully meditative state, not unlike the blissful mental escape I'd experience whenever I'd pop off to "Switzerland." The "glam squad" would swoop in and go about transforming me into Kelly Taylor, a process that took a lot longer than you'd think. I'd take this time to learn my lines and bring my focus back to work. And just when I'd begin to feel like my old, professional self, my mommy alarm would clang and I'd beg for a quick break so I could dash out to the RV to feed, change, or just eyeball and kiss Luca Bella; then I'd dash back to makeup, hustle back into my chair, and we'd pick up where we left off. And just as quickly as I'd snapped out of my makeup-induced reverie, I'd be back, almost nodding off, filled with gratitude for the rest this time gave me.

I swear to God, I was bringing a whole new meaning to the concept of work/mommy balance, and the proof was in the path I was beating from the studio out to the trailer, a few yards of concrete that I probably wore down to nothing, given that I made the trip about a thousand times a day.

And I have to give it up to the glam squad, the crew, and everyone on set: They were incredibly patient with me while I figured all this new-mom stuff out. I was well aware of this generosity, so I did what I could to bring my best game to work, to be on time, prepared, and as ready, willing, and able as possible.

While I was adjusting to being back at work, Luca Bella was doing what babies do: She was becoming cuter and chunkier and more delightful by the day. As she grew, we expanded her world accordingly. The set designers were always sprucing up the RV by doing incredibly sweet things, like adding an AstroTurf lawn and a white picket fence. I have a dear friend, my first mommy friend, a woman named Andy, whom I met in a Billy Blanks Tae Bo class. There I was in his gym, faux-kickboxing in an effort to shed the last vestiges of my baby weight, while Luca was in the room next door, playing baby games with other Tae Bo kids. After class one day, Andy, who'd had a baby girl right around the time I'd had Luca, zoomed in on me and decided we were going to be friends. She'd come out to the set with her sweet daughter, and we would fill a kiddie pool with water and watch our babies splash and play, and at times our RV with its little front yard would feel like an actual home. When Luca was big enough, Nina would bring her onto the set after her naps, and I'd get to hug her and squeeze her before she'd be passed around like a beautiful, sweet-smelling football. (It's amazing what the presence of a supercute baby can do to defuse workplace politicking: Suddenly whatever was causing so much stress vanishes and everyone is smiling—at least as long as the kid is within sight.) She was with me for those long days for three years, and while she was cutting her teeth, learning to crawl, then walk, and then learning to speak, I was working. I remember one day, after a couple of years of our routine, realizing that little Luca had actually spent more time on set than she had at home. Talk about being a working girl.

I guess that means that showbiz really is in her genes.

As for me, to this day, I find sitting in a makeup chair to be an incredibly relaxing and restorative experience. So much so that recently, when a healer asked me to envision a safe place, I closed my eyes and thought about a makeup department, a place that was stocked with pots of foundation, tubes of lipstick, and trays of brightly colored eye shadow. And just as I would be drifting off to a happier place, a pair of hands brandishing a giant blush brush in one hand, a powder puff in the other, would be moving in close.

Ah, heaven.

LEAVING THE ZIP CODE

The end of *90210* was so many things to me. On the one hand, it was a huge relief; I mean, we'd been on the air for ten years. Ten. Freaking. Years. By the time Donna and David walked down that aisle and Dylan and Kelly were back together, I was chasing after a three-year-old. The vast disconnect between my real life and Kelly Taylor's life was almost comical at that point, except for the fact that *90210* was not a comedy; it was a drama, and Kelly Taylor had lived through every trauma a harried team of Hollywood writers could dream up. Let's see, off the top of my head, the character I played had been shot, addicted to cocaine, addicted to diet pills, trapped in a burning building, and then terribly scarred. She'd also been in a cult, held at gunpoint by a lesbian stalker who wanted to be her, almost raped by a cowboy, and . . . I'm sure I'm forgetting your personal favorite calamity, but you get the point: As Kelly Taylor, I was just all cried out, so leaving her behind was almost a relief.

But, man, saying good-bye to the cast and crew? That was a whole other story, given that we had been with one another day in and day out for those long and developmentally important adolescent and early adult years. Shannen, Luke, Jason, Tori, Ian, Brian, Gabrielle, and I had all grown up together. We were, in some ways, more like siblings than just friends, having walked through so much with one another. By the time the show ended, we'd been to one another's weddings (at least a few of us had been married, and, in my case, divorced), and I'd gone ahead and broken the baby-making ground.

Throughout the filming of the show and afterward, we had an unspoken pact that we would do our best not to act out and misbehave the way young stars are prone to do, and that we'd take care of one another, that we'd have one another's backs. And we meant it: Not one of us ever went off the rails, and this says something about what kind of people my castmates are, what kind of bond we had. Our loyalty is just as solid today as it was in 1990.

But all good things come to an end, and it was time, finally, for us to leave the Peach Pit, and Beverly High, and the angst and drama and sparkly sunshine behind. It was time to give up my parking spot and my cozy little dressing room–slash-cubicle and to pack up my awesome baby trailer. It was time for me, for all of us, to get on with life.

One of the things I did right away was dye my hair dark brown. I don't know if this was a symbolic gesture, a way of washing Kelly Taylor out of my hair once and for all, so to speak. But I wanted to find out what it was like to live on the "darker" side, to give up my blond identity while I retreated from the spotlight and thought about what I wanted to do next.

Becoming a brunette gave me a level of anonymity I'd never experienced before. It was as though I'd joined the witness protection program or something: I could go places and not be recognized. I could talk to strangers now, without being asked for an autograph. I didn't get constantly hit on either, which was a good thing, because I was madly in love and recently engaged. All in all, becoming a brunette was a pretty wonderfully liberating experience.

The only person who wasn't loving the darker shade was Mr. Showbiz. He could not get anyone interested in a brunette Jennie Garth, which struck me as absurd and silly, because they were hiring me, right? . . . not my blondeness. Or so I wanted to believe, but I was wrong. I was a blonde through and through. It got to the point where Mr. Showbiz told me to just call him when I went back to my roots, and finally I did. But not before heading down to the DMV and getting a new picture taken for my driver's license—as a brunette. I also had a picture taken and had it blown up and framed, and presented it to Mr. Showbiz the next time I saw him, because I know how much it bugs him, seeing me with brown hair, and I just love pushing his buttons.

It was time to get real. Time to get back to work. And time to get on with the rest of my blond life.

I knew I didn't want to take on anything that would take me away from Peter and Luca, so feature films were out, because doing film work usually requires traveling to far-off locations for months at a time. I landed a recurring role in a new drama, *The $treet*, but it would be shot in New York, which didn't feel so far away. Plus, we had Peter's family there. So I packed up baby Luca, and my mom came along to act as nanny, and off to the Big Apple we went. It was quite a bonding adventure for us girls! The production rented us an apartment in the superswanky Trump building overlooking the Hudson River. It sounded great, but in reality being over on the West Side Highway was like being in a wind tunnel. Plus, it was the dead of winter, and my call times were, of course, at the crack of dawn, so I'd be standing in front of my building, trying to hail a cab just before rush hour hit. It was freezing cold and I was freshly showered and all moisturized and dewy, and the first bus that would pass by would blow up a cloud of authentic New

York City street grime. I'd show up on set looking like I'd been out all night, and the makeup people would shake their heads while they scrubbed the MTA grime off of me. The show was about a group of gorgeous, horny Wall Streeters and was created by my friend Darren Star, the brilliant mind behind *Sex and the City* and *Beverly Hills, 90210*. I got to play a really bad girl who was the sister of one of the brokers, and who got into a steamy tryst with a rich guy played by Bradley Cooper. We'd be setting up for a sex scene, lying in the set bed, and he'd be asking me what it was like to be engaged or what it was like living with someone and having a child. Then we'd get ready to do a take and the next thing you know, I'm making out with him. Or I'd be shooting the breeze with another hot young actor while everyone was bustling around and working, and then we would gear up for yet another steamy scene. It was a great job, but only one season was ever shot, and only part of that season was ever aired. Turns out that was just enough for me. I was ready to get back to warm and friendly and less grimy LA, and back to my life with my family, and readjusting to being a "civilian" after the long, rigorous march of *90210*. I kind of liked the quiet; it gave me time to think—and to plan a wedding.

BUILDING OUR BOAT

Peter and I had definitely taken the road less traveled. First came love, for sure, but instead of marriage, we had jumped right to the baby carriage. Now, I can't see doing it any other way, not only because having Luca was the best thing that had happened to both of us, but because it gave us the time, as Peter used to say, to "build our boat." This meant that we took our time to work on creating a relationship, a family, that would have staying power. And we were, by the time *90210* wrapped, doing a pretty good job of it.

When he proposed to me, I knew that it meant so much to him, to us—more than I can even describe here. It was so much about our both wanting to stand before our families, not only in honor of each other, but in honor of them, and to acknowledge how gratefully interconnected we felt. Getting married was a decision that I knew took Peter a while to come to. I knew he had given it so much thought and consideration. I took this really seriously and even converted to Catholicism so we could have a traditional Catholic wedding mass.

I loved the planning of it. I decided on a white-and-deep-red theme. We decided to make the wedding something of a "queen's affair," because Peter had three older sisters serving as his attendants that day, and I had three of my sisters attending me. The half dozen sisters were joined by his three best childhood friends, and Tori and Tiffani and Andy, my best mom-friend, rounded out our dozen by serving as my bridesmaids. They all looked so gorgeous in their strapless deep-ruby-red gowns.

I loved my dress, a stunning creation by the designer Reem Acra. My dress was so dramatic, especially the train, which was superlong and embellished with a huge, hand-stitched silver cross at the bottom. It had a swooping, off-the-shoulder neckline that was so romantic. Sweet Luca would also be wearing a Reem Acra gown that had been custom-made for her to match mine. I knew Peter would love this.

But even more dramatic was my hair, which had been shot through with chunks of honey brown. It was piled on my head in a way that seemed to take many of our guests by surprise. It was edgy and unexpected and daring, which was just what I wanted to complement my traditional gown. I loved it! But it did, I'll admit, look a bit like my hairstylist, Kelly, had set a fountain on the top of my head.

Luca looked like an angel that had dropped straight down from heaven. She had her luscious ringlets set just so, and her dress was adorned with a deep red sash, the same color as the bridesmaids' dresses. She solemnly carried a small wicker basket filled with fresh red rose petals. Just as she was about to make her way down the aisle, the priest told her not to just strew the petals along the white runner, but to actually hand a petal to each of our one hundred and fifty guests. Luca took this job quite seriously, and this meant those little fingers took one red rose petal out of that basket at a time. This took great concentration on her part, and I watched, my heart breaking with the overwhelming adorableness of her, as she carefully chose each rose petal and then handed them off: "Here's one for you, Uncle Bob; one for you, the lady in the hat I don't know; one for you, Kevin Spacey, since you just worked with Daddy; one for you, Jason Priestley, because I've known you since before I was born." I just watched her in awe and tried to be patient, because it took her a good ten minutes to make it to the altar.

And then, when she finally got there . . . my dad took my hand. Yes! He had miraculously made it to wedding number two. He was a little wobbly, for sure, but he looked so handsome and debonair in his bespoke suit. I rested my hand on his arm and we began our slow walk down the aisle. I was in tears before I was even halfway to the altar. It just overwhelmed me how beautiful and serene the church was, how everyone we loved best in the world was there, holding their breath with such fierce love as I made my way to Peter, who was looking at me with such intensity. Though there was a moment, strangely, when I looked over at him during one of the readings and I noticed that he was looking off into the far distance, with a focus on something that was way, way beyond where we were. I remember wondering, just for a split second, where he was. But that moment passed, and when we came together, face-to-face to say our vows, we held each other's hands tenderly and tight. At one point I began to cry again, and I dropped my tissue down into the bodice of my gown, and without missing a beat, Peter took the handkerchief out of his breast pocket and dried my eyes. It was one of those moments, the kind you never forget.

Our reception was a rocking, relaxed party, and I'm pretty certain everyone had a great time. My favorite moment? Dancing with Peter, Luca held between us, the three of us laughing so hard. We were like the Three Musketeers, ready to embark on life's next great adventure. Together.

Our boat was built. And there, in that idyllic little chapel, we had just set sail.

ALL ABOARD!

was stoked about my life. And now I was stoked about work again. I'd just heard from my friend Peter Roth, the head of Warner Bros. Studios, that the pilot of a new comedy that I'd lobbied hard for, and which he'd had the faith to cast me in, was going to be picked up. The show was called *What I Like About You*, and costarred a talented young actress, Amanda Bynes. This news meant we would be going into a full season's production, and Peter Roth wanted me to appear at the "upfronts" in New York, where the show would be unveiled. The upfronts are a lavish series of events where the networks release their fall lineups and trot out some of their stars. Advertisers clamor for airspace on the "hot" shows, and there's a feeding frenzy of deal making, parties, and press appearances. All in all, it's a pretty great time.

And I was feeling great, too! I was in smoking-hot shape, having finally gotten my body back after baby number one; my little family was going to travel with me; and, it's worth mentioning, I was finally back to being blond. It's no coincidence that I landed *What I Like About You* as soon as I gave up the brunette experiment. Knowing I was about to begin a great full-time gig meant it was the perfect time for us to take a trip east: We'd both get in some business and we'd get to spend time with Peter's family. We were ready. *Let's do this. Let's get on that train!*

Train, you say?

Peter and I were still in the middle of our "no airplanes for us" phase that we'd adopted right after 9/11. Plus, we took Luca with us wherever we went, and somehow or another we'd gotten all goo-goo eyed and romantic about taking the train across the country. I fantasized about our being tucked into a sleeping birth that was romantically cramped, like the train car that Eva Marie Saint and Cary Grant steamed up in *North by Northwest*, except ours would have a wee trundle bed in it for Luca. We'd feel like pioneers, making our way across this great land of ours, and we'd marvel, in awe, at all of the beauty around us.

I guess I should have been tipped off by the brochure Peter shared with me:

"Save money and make memories when you take the kids on a journey they won't soon forget. They'll take in the wonder and fun of the train, while you enjoy a trip without baggage fees and traffic stops. So whether gazing out the window or cuddled up with a book or movie, the fun just keeps on going."

And let me tell you, the fun really did just keep on going. Just before we were set to depart, I found out that we would be traveling with a stowaway: I was pregnant! Little Lola would be on board too . . . in my belly.

Now we had all the more reason to celebrate—we would spend five glorious days together, taking in all that wonder; then we'd land and get to share our fabulous news with the Facinelli side of the family.

But here's what that brochure failed to mention. The "wonder" is how they cleverly design those family cars. This sleeper car included a couch and chair, and when you lifted the cushion on the chair—voilà!—there was your own private commode! There was a sizable gap between the bottom of the cushion and the metal bowl, so the pleasant aroma of whatever your family member had deposited could swirl and waft into the four-by-four space we were now trapped in.

What's even worse—especially if you're newly pregnant and your senses of smell and taste have become super X-ray sensitive—was that these very seats would become our beds at night. This meant that while we rested, our heads were just inches above the cesspool beneath that cushion. I'm sure you're not surprised to learn that, given that our "family car" smelled faintly like the restroom at a truck stop before we even got settled in, and once we figured out why, we all opted to use the more public restrooms on the train.

In fact, we spent very little time in our "family" car, and chose instead to roam the train, exploring. For me, this meant searching for food, and let me tell you, it is not very easy to find something fresh and nutritious on a vehicle that is chugging through shockingly vast empty swaths of our country. I'm a pretty picky eater to begin with, and I'm largely vegetarian, so eating on that train turned out to be one of the great unplanned "fasts" of my life. I don't mean to be unkind, but the food on that train, which was all shrink-wrapped and slightly soggy, made McDonald's seem downright free-range fresh, and so I tended to nibble on whatever fresh fruit I could scrounge up.

We would, however, stop from time to time, so they could change engines and so we passengers could step off and take in a bit of fresh air. Once, somewhere in the middle of the country, as soon as I stepped off the train, I smelled popcorn. There! Across the tracks, tucked into a strip mall, was a movie theater. Without a thought, I just all-out sprinted across those train tracks and ran into that movie theater and ordered a large popcorn, extra butter and salt. It was the best meal I had during those five days.

And then there was the sleeping part of it all. I've already let you in on the little under-the-mattress-there's-a-toilet secret, but then there was the challenge of actually sleeping on a moving train. I don't know why it was, but during the day, the train seemed to meander across the land at a lovely, just-right pace that felt almost kind of hypnotic and dreamy. But at night? That's when I guess they made up for all the time they lost driving at a reasonable pace during the day, because all of a sudden, almost as soon as the sun went down, they floored it and you found yourself kind of hanging on for dear life while the train transformed into a giant metal heat-seeking missile that was hell-bent on reaching its target. The *clickety-clack* of the wheels on the tracks became an incessant clanging, and the cars moaned and buckled and swayed like mad against the crazy velocity. Trying to sleep while all this was going on defied the body's logic, which was convinced you were on a runaway death trap and so was constantly braced for impact. Peter and I would clutch on to each other, snuggled up under the twenty-thread-count sheets imprinted with the train logo, our heads perched at unnatural angles on those rock-hard, yet crunchy pillows, our eyes wide and unblinking, locked on each other with an "I hope we get out of this alive" intensity. It was probably a good thing that the rocketing train was so loud that we couldn't talk; otherwise, we'd have been screaming for our lives. Of course, little Luca managed to sleep like a rock, and I remember feeling relieved when dawn would break and I could see the sky again.

Despite the fact that those five days felt like fifty, we did make it to New York alive, a little ragged and wrinkled, and more than a little motion sick, but happy to be back on Peter's home turf and in the bosom of his big, loving Italian family. They loved it when they got to see us, especially Luca, and they were all over the moon with our news about *bambino numero due.*

While my family was nestled into our larger family, I got to glam all up and strut my stuff at all of these fancy "upfront" parties and events, and it felt great to hear how excited the execs and the advertisers and all the rest of the players in the television universe were about our show. And all this positive feedback was a very good thing, because I still had to tell my bosses about my pregnancy, and I wanted to do so in the least disruptive way possible, especially since I'd be playing a single gal who lives with her younger sister. I knew my bosses weren't going to be thrilled about my news the way Peter's *nonna* was; that's for sure. But what was a girl to do?

WHAT I LIKE ABOUT YOU

After all the drama Kelly Taylor went through, I just didn't want to be so serious anymore. I actually wanted to laugh and make people laugh, so I decided comedy ought to be my next move. I got on the phone with Mr. Showbiz and said, "Start sending me out on meetings for a comedy, a sitcom; I'm ready to make people laugh." To which he replied, "Okay. But . . . can you be funny?"

It turns out Mr. Showbiz wasn't the only one asking this question—even I wanted to know. So every night, after Luca went to bed, I started watching sitcoms like crazy, tuning in nightly to reruns of *Friends* or *Everybody Loves Raymond* or *Will & Grace*. I wasn't watching for the escapism or even the laughs; I was watching it in order to crack the code and get a sense of the rhythm of it all. I wanted to absorb as much as I could about what made a comedy work. To Mr. Showbiz's credit, he got me an audition pretty quickly, but it did not go as well as we'd hoped, and let me tell you, there is nothing funny about a bad audition—well, at least if it's yours. For me, I can tell I'm tanking when I start to sweat like a pig—the flop sweats. It's the worst. You're trapped in a room with a casting director, maybe some executives, and you're horrifyingly aware of how bad you are sucking, and your fight-or-flight instinct kicks in, but I was just too earnest, too serious, to stop the audition and say, "Wait. This was a bad idea." There was too much Kelly Taylor in that room with me; I was just too tightly wound.

My next audition came around, and straight to the comedy coach I went. Together we broke the scenes down line by line, talked endlessly about the characteristics that made my character say the things she did, and worked on how much faster the delivery is when you're riffing with someone else for laughs.

I was twenty-nine at the time, and had been "unemployed" for about a year. By unemployed, I mean I was working; I just wasn't signed up for a recurring role in an established series, like I had been for so, so long. And consequently, for the first time since I'd landed in Hollywood, I felt a bit discouraged. Before I could get too down in the dumps, though, Mr. Showbiz called to say a full-on offer had come in for me to star opposite the teen sensation Amanda Bynes in a half-hour comedy. I was stoked! And more than a bit surprised, because I still, to this day, have no idea why they took a bet on an actress with absolutely zero comedy experience.

A few days later, I met with Amanda and the producers, and it felt like my first day on *90210* when we did a table reading of the script. I felt a little awkward and a bit uncomfortable, as though somehow they knew, before they even met me, that they'd hired the wrong girl. But things went well and they felt good enough about my odds to hire me on to film the pilot.

We shot the pilot for *What I Like About You* in March 2002. I remember this because it was right before my thirtieth birthday, which coincidentally was also Amanda's sixteenth birthday. When you share a birth date with someone, you are kind of karmic "twins," and you auto-matically have a certain unspoken bond, just like the bond I shared with my father, who was also an April 3 baby. To celebrate our joint "big day," the producers brought in a huge cake with both of our faces reproduced in frosting on it. It was a great way to start a new job, and it's a birthday I will never forget.

We'd been cooped up on Soundstage 25 on the Warner Bros. lot for two weeks, prepping to shoot the pilot. In that short amount of time, I learned that comedy is way more demanding than drama. You have to be present, nimble, and ready. I felt like a featherweight prizefighter training for some big fight. There was a "training" schedule, if you will, and it ran on a weekly production clock. On the first day of the week we'd get the script, and we'd all sit around a big table and read through it. We all would read our respective parts—me, Amanda, Wesley Jona-than, Simon Rex, Leslie Grossman, and Allison Munn. Plus whatever guest stars were involved that week. The writers needed to hear their words out loud so they could tell if the jokes were working and if the dialogue was flowing and hanging together. It was all out there, and so if a joke bombed—or if one of us bombed in the telling of it—a note would be taken and we'd move on. I would get a little self-conscious, a little shaky in the knees, whenever my lines came up, having that same kind of terrified sense of anticipation you might have when it was your turn to talk in front of the whole class.

I learned pretty quickly that read-throughs are where it's at: If you didn't hit it then, you might be taken out of a scene, or at least your joke might be. So there was a level of energy to the performance, even at that early stage, that was crucial to the success of the whole. I found it pretty exhilarating. And I didn't want to screw up and have my lines cut or be rewritten for a funnier actor.

I loved my character, Val Tyler, too. She was super-high-strung and very OCD and was always trying to be in charge of her younger, more erratic little sister. This was my first time playing the "older" person on a show, the "parent" part, if you will. And now, I was the more seasoned actor on set, with years of experience under my belt. The unpredictable-teenager part was now being played flawlessly by the lovely and incredibly professional Amanda. I feel so grateful that she was such a pro, because the truth is, I hadn't really spent any time around teenagers, and because of my experiences with them as fans, they kind of freaked me out a little. Plus, for most of my life I'd always been surrounded by adults, so being around an actual child actor was pretty eye-opening, and it made me feel less fearful about what I'd bump up against once my Luca reached her teens.

Once we'd tackled the table read, the writers would go back to their lair and we actors would get to work, putting the show "on its feet." This meant starting at the top and working through the whole show scene by scene. There was a lot of blocking out of movement and intricate staging for everything that was on the page.

After that first day, I felt like I was working on the moon. Here we were, all of us huddled up on this giant, cavernous, cold soundstage with construction going on all around us, while the crew began to build whatever sets were needed for that week. There was the hum of these giant overhead fluorescent lights that cast a strange green glow over all of us. The director and his assistant and script supervisor all huddled in front of the set, watching us closely and offering guidance here and there.

It was strange doing that walk-through, telling jokes one after another—but no one was laughing; only the stage crickets were chirping. That was because everyone was too busy working away on their own piece of the puzzle, and at that early point in the week, it was still a long way from coming together. The goal was to have the whole thing up and running pretty smoothly by the end of the second day of rehearsals. Then, the producers and writers would all come back and watch a run-through of the entire show. For this, the stage was suddenly awash in pretty warm light, and there was laughter everywhere. It felt kind of like doing a play, but instead of being in seats, the audience was standing two feet from you, arms folded, eyes glued to the clipboards in their hands, pencils at the ready. It was pretty intense actually, and it took some time for me to adjust to how "out there" all of this was, how you could be running your lines, and then one of the dozens of people milling around you might cough or laugh or take a call, and you'd have to block it out and keep going. You learned pretty quickly that you had to take an extra breath after you delivered a joke, so that the laughter could kick in. The crew around us would always laugh at those moments, but in this mechanical "ha-ha" way. It was strange. It was messy. It was so, so different from the controlled, closed set of *90210*. It was fun. But it was also scary as hell stepping out there in those lights, putting yourself in front of all those people, and really throwing caution to the wind. To do comedy you have to really go for it! To be fully willing to look like a big boob, to be okay trying anything just to get that laugh. This took me really getting over myself; I had to be comfortable being vulnerable like that, and to be ready to fail, and to try again and again. I can remember during the first live taping, with the studio audience sitting expectantly in their stadium-style chairs, I wasn't letting go; I wasn't fully committing to being as ridiculous as necessary. The executive producer and cocreator of the show, Wil Calhoun, took me aside and pleaded with me to trust him; he told me he wouldn't let me fail, and that I *had* to step outside my comfort zone. His commitment to me and the intense honesty I felt in that moment sort of fired me up. I felt safe to go back out there onstage and give it more than I ever knew I could.

I learned how to "hold for the laugh." You know, that fake sitcom laughter that bursts forth whenever a joke is told. It was canned, of course, and if the joke was big, the laugh track was loud and a little more sustained. If the joke was small, they'd roll out more of a chuckle. There was a rhythm to this hilarity that revealed itself to me pretty quickly, and once I got into the groove, I realized there was some wisdom in learning to hold for the laugh. It kind of made things . . . nicer. So next time you're in a group and you say something clever, remember to hold for the laugh. And think of me.

Spending five days a week on a soundstage with an ensemble makes for fast and fond bonding. Everything was close by: our dressing rooms, and the commissary where we usually ate lunch together. I grew to like being the older one, and felt real motherly, big-sisterly affection for sweet Amanda, who was so real and down-to-earth and so normal and bubbly and excited by life. It was refreshing to be around her energy. She took pleasure in having her hair curled just so, or she'd be excited about a cool new nail polish. She wasn't at all vapid or shallow; she was alive and young and exactly the way she was supposed to be. Especially given that she had lived most of her life so deeply embedded in the microcosm of the entertainment industry. She'd starred in her own show, on Nickelodeon, since she was about ten years old. Many, many adults made a living because of her, and knowing this always raised the red flag for me. I'd been there, too, but I was older than she was now when I'd started. I couldn't imagine what all that pressure would do to a preteen psyche. But, of course, at least outwardly it didn't affect her; she'd dance around with abandon when her favorite song came on the radio, and you could tell she just needed to expel all that pent-up teen energy. The director and whoever else was rehearsing with her would step back and let her do her thing for a few minutes, or if the mood struck, we'd join her and laugh and soak up all of her youthfulness. Free. Uncomplicated. Easy. That's how I would describe Amanda. I can honestly credit her with changing my perspective on teenagers. She made me love young people in a whole new way, to really see them and embrace and respect their blossoming individuality, rather than being afraid of or put off by it. And now with my Luca, who just turned sixteen, I am able to really look at her and love every moment of who she is—all because of Amanda. She taught me to notice what I like about you—even when it's crazy, angsty, dramatic teenage stuff.

I loved my four years on that show. Everyone was incredibly gracious and supportive of me while I learned the ropes, and especially during that very first season, when I was not only the newbie, but I was pregnant. I will never forget how wonderful Peter Roth was when I broke the news to him, right after the upfronts and the news that the show had been picked up. He couldn't have been more gracious and supportive, and fortunately for all of us, though Lola turned out to be a pretty good-size baby, she was a really compact bump, so hiding her wasn't that difficult. Plus, the costumers on the show were both moms and so they "got it," and they happily and very artfully concealed my, ahem, girth. I was on my feet most of the workday now, and when I started to get puffy, swollen ankles, Rebecca, the coolest assistant director you could ever hope to work with, would push me around the set in a chair on casters, just to give me a few moments off my feet. As my pregnancy progressed, the writers just seemed to naturally write more of the pratfalls and physical comedy for the other actors, and I spent more and more scenes leaning against the kitchen counter or sitting and reading, usually with a newspaper, which is the best bump cover-up going. There was only ever one pregnancy "incident," and it involved me, a rug, and a wooden springboard.

We were shooting in front of a live audience, and in this one scene, Amanda would vault over the couch by launching herself from a springboard that was hidden under a rug behind the living room couch. Well, before Amanda could launch herself, I waddled in on cue, my character, Val, scolding her character, Holly, about something or other, and I proceeded to trip right over the rigged-up carpet and went down like a 747 with engine failure. Everything went silent while I rolled over and scrambled back up to my feet. I was fine. The baby was fine. But it sure scared the hell out of everybody, especially the studio audience.

Coincidentally, just like with Luca's birth, Lola was due right at the end of that first-season shooting schedule. We wrapped right before Thanksgiving, and she came on December 6, 2002. Wow! To think: By the time she was born, Lola Ray had already traveled across the country by train and starred on a sitcom! Her life was off to a great start, and she came out so fat and round and perfect, with a red birthmark on her forehead that would get redder whenever she cried, which was close to never. She was (and still is) the absolute spitting image of my dad: blond and robust and utterly lovable. And thank God, because her big sister, Luca, who had been an only child for a good five years before Lola was born, and who hadn't been that excited about becoming a big sister, adored her. Life was good!

What I Like About You was a fantastic work experience. It allowed me to work "in town" and be with my growing family, and I felt truly liberated doing comedy. I loved my colleagues, especially Amanda, and I loved freeing up that part of me that never saw the light of day on *90210*. It definitely helped me stretch and grow, not just as an actress, but as a mother, a woman, a person. It was simply a really great gig.

RV'ING

I've got a deep, deep love of all things RV. It probably started with my dad's old crappy camper collection. When I was a kid, from time to time he'd pull into the driveway behind the wheel of yet another dilapidated used recreational vehicle, the wild look of satisfaction from another successful acquisition gleaming in his eye. He loved nothing better than cramming all six of us into his old blue Ford pickup truck and hitting the open road. He and my mom would ride up in the cab, and all of us kids would be in the back of the pickup having a free-for-all under the camper cap that was haphazardly mounted above us. Pillows were swinging, potato chips were flying, game cards were being thrown down. My parents would say the best part of the vacation was the driving, because it was the one time they'd get some peace and quiet and be able to spend some time alone together. I guess they couldn't hear all the screaming and racket that was going on the back.

Spending long family trips trapped in that tiny camper with my older sisters made me want to re-create this experience for my own kids. I bought my first RV and introduced Luca to RV life when I set up our home away from home in an RV on the *90210* lot so I could bring Luca to work with me. But Peter had the RV bug, too, and so we started renting them, not sure whether we would ever feel brave enough to make the huge investment in the kind of tricked-out rig we lusted after. But after Fiona, our youngest, was born, we bought our own forty-foot diesel pusher with four slide-outs, and we parked it right out in front of our big hoity-toity house in Toluca Lake, which is one of the tonier enclaves of LA. Man, our neighbors were not happy with that thing—but I was. I had it loaded up with every creature comfort, every imaginable thing we would ever need. It was locked and loaded! This was the dream; now we could just hop in and hit the road whenever we wanted to.

Now, Peter is a guy who loves his cars, but being from New York . . . I'm trying to figure out how to say this as diplomatically as possible: He is a *terrible driver*. I mean, just being in the passenger seat of a Toyota Camry with him can be a harrowing experience. Being in a giant motor home with him at the wheel is an experience like no other. I would have to literally sit on my hands to keep myself from gesticulating wildly, like a crazy driver's ed teacher who thinks that somehow she can actually drive if she waves her hands spastically in the air. My anxiety around his driving got so bad that I would take my anxiety medication before we'd hit the road, and we even went to couples' therapy for this very issue, as my backseat driving—my inability to keep my mouth shut while he took turns too fast or tailgated the cars ahead of us—would cause a bit too much friction in our marriage.

So while I was biting my tongue, we'd be driving along, and all the drivers around us would be cursing and flipping Peter off, and I remember Luca saying, "Why are all the people yelling at us, Daddy? And why are they putting their fingers up?" And Peter and I would just smile and he'd say, "Oh, those are my friends and they're just saying hello!" And he'd give them all a big wave back and shout, "Hello!" and we'd just barrel on down the road, terrorizing everyone within miles. It was in those moments—when I would be struggling and stewing and Peter would be silly and devil-may-care and he'd make me laugh and then it just didn't seem like we were going to die—that I'd relax. We always got there in one piece. We never had an accident. And every time we took a trip, he'd be the lovable doofus dad at the wheel, like Chevy Chase in *Vacation*. So with the help of a few shrinks, and the realization that his goofy, slightly dangerous driving humor was actually good for me, I learned to mostly let go and let him have his way behind the wheel.

We were one of those families who liked to go off the beaten path and find a KOA site somewhere in the middle of nowhere, where we could park and set up our home away from home. Most of the memories we made on these trips were fond ones, but one time there was a dumping incident that, when I think about it, still makes me shudder. I don't have any recollection of what state we were in, and maybe that's a good thing, because if I did, I might never go back there.

I do know, though, that we were in our big-ass fancy rig, making a cross-country trek, and whenever we'd pull into some ragtag RV overnight site, we'd get a lot of attention. Usually, because people would come over to check out the rig, they'd figure out pretty quickly that we were celebrity types from Hollywood, and the buzz would race through the campground. There would be whispers at the swing sets, or long glances when I went to the general store to pick up toilet paper and toothpaste. People would go quiet when we'd approach a fire pit after dark, eager to roast a few wieners and marshmallows for ourselves, too. The more the hullabaloo, the shyer I'd become, and before you knew it, I was hiding out behind our little RV curtains, busying myself at the miniature sink while Peter and the girls were out and about. In the end, I didn't really mind much, as I actually enjoy cleaning and cooking, but

I would sometimes finish all my work and sit and stare out the window and wonder what kind of fun they were having out there. At those moments, I felt like a total campground weirdo.

At the end of this visit, we made our usual stop at the "dump station," which is where you go to empty the gray and black water from your holding tanks. The gray water is the sink and shower water; the black water is the toilet water. If you've seen the movie *RV* with Robin Williams, you have a better understanding of this whole dump situation, and how complicated and gross it can be. Being the decent man that he is, Peter always took on this unpleasant task. After this one stop, I'm not exactly sure what happened, but apparently he didn't quite get the hose hooked up tight enough to our tanks or something, and there was some kind of backup or spill, and instead of going into the septic tank, our black water ran all over the concrete area just in front of the general store. The on-site manager came running out and I slid open the window to see what the hell was going on. There was Peter, dancing all around, his giant rubber gloves no longer helpful at this point, and he just flashed a huge smile at this livid guy and said, "I do *not* know what the hell my wife ate last night!" The guy stopped, looked at Peter, then looked up at the window and saw me, the mysterious "famous" lady from slot seventeen, looking back at him. Then he seemed to figure out that I apparently was the one who'd caused this calamity. I swear, if I didn't love Peter so much, I would have killed him then, and many other times, when he would set me up like that.

Just this last year, since the split with Peter, I took the girls on a cross-country trip. My brother Chuck joined us for some of the journey, and my assistant Liz met up with us for a few days, too. I think I wanted to prove to myself that I could do it on my own, that I didn't need a man to continue this "family" tradition. And I did it. I did all the driving. All the cooking. All the navigating. And all the dumping.

We had a great time and visited lots of friends and family.

But if I'm being honest with myself—which is the point of this whole thing, isn't it?—I did miss having Peter along. His sense of adventure, coupled with his devil-may-care attitude, always kept me on my toes. Always snapped me back into the present and out of myself.

As a result of the divorce, we sold the RV and everything in it. Someone recently asked me if I thought I'd ever get another one. I honestly don't have an answer to that question. I guess time will tell, but for now I sure do have a lot of great RV memories.

SO YOU THINK I CAN DANCE?

In the spring of 2006, I was having the time of my life. *What I Like About You* had wrapped after four seasons about a year before. The timing of the show's end was perfect, momentous even, because it meant that I could just relax for once and enjoy my pregnancy. That's right: I got pregnant for the third time just as the show wrapped. For the first time in three pregnancies I didn't have to show up at work and worry about how well my bump would be hidden, or contend with the poor wardrobe people who would be dreading dressing my ballooning body. I cannot overstate what a huge relief this was. I was able to spend my pregnancy eating whatever I wanted. I could finally let it all hang out. It was awesome.

Fiona came along in the fall of 2006, and with her arrival, I found myself just sinking into an indescribably joyful and contented state of family bliss. Life was quiet in a way that I found so fantastic, because it was actually anything but quiet: It was filled with squealing and laughing and lots of running of little feet (our girls were active!). I had three little ducklings—two of whom were in constant motion and one of whom was not yet walking, but eager to keep up with her older sisters. Talk about girl power. We were rockin' it at our house. And I was loving it.

The quiet I'm talking about came from the fact that I was on a work hiatus for the first time in a long, long time. There were no meetings, no long days on set. No hair and makeup. And I was so content in my little family bubble. It was pretty great.

But then . . . as it tends to do . . .

The phone rang.

In good conscience, I can't blame this one on Mr. Showbiz, though I wish I could, of course. No, this one I have to blame on those crafty producers from *Dancing with the Stars*, who have the uncanny ability to track down sedentary celebrities who have recently fallen completely off the radar—and I was, at that point, definitely one of those. It was nice that they called, but in all honesty, I did not want to be found. And I definitely did not want to dance—I just wanted to sleep (as any mother of three under the age of ten would; maybe there's a show in that concept—*Sleeping In with the Stars?*).

But once I started talking to them, I knew I was in trouble. I'm one who never shies away from any professional challenge that rattles my comfort zone, so the idea of dancing in front of a live audience totally intrigued me in a completely horrifying way. This assignment would be the opposite experience of acting on a closed sound stage; in fact, it wouldn't be about acting at all. This meant training six to eight hours a day, putting on ballroom dancing shoes and a custom-sewn BeDazzled gown, and strutting your stuff—on a stage, live, in front of lots and lots and lots of people. I mean, what could possibly be better, right?

Then I started getting texts from Ian Ziering, who'd just wrapped his own stint on *DWTS*, making it to the semifinals and placing a respectable fourth on season four. He was so encouraging ("Do it! Do it! Do it!") that I found myself giving it serious thought.

But I agonized, of course, and consulted with my "team," which included Mr. Showbiz, Adele, and my husband, who would have to hold down the fort at home. But finally, in the end, after way too much hemming and hawing, there was no reason not to do it, so I signed on. And once I did, that good old feeling of absolute dread washed over me, just like it had back when I was fourteen and had signed up for that Cinderella-y pageant where I'd gotten to dance in front of an audience and a panel of judges. I mean, who says fantasies about becoming a ballerina die just because you're the mother of three, over thirty-five, and not in great shape?

It seemed like within minutes of saying yes, this extremely young, fresh-faced guy showed up at my door, camera crew in tow. It was Derek Hough, who was joining the pro team of *DWTS* that season, and I would be his very first partner. Derek had just flown back from London, where he'd finished a run as Ren in *Footloose* onstage in the West End. He was all of twenty-two, I think, sweet and kind, and my three girls followed him out to our backyard like puppies, bumping into one another trying not to bump into him. We sat and chatted awkwardly, and I remember thinking, *Does he even have facial hair yet?* And so I'd move in a little closer, kind of amazed at the fact that he was so young.

Every time Derek made a gesture or opened his mouth, my kids giggled. In fact, there were fits of giggles. I could tell they thought he was the most adorable thing they'd ever laid eyes on, like a teddy bear just pulled down from a high shelf. I'm pretty sure they were in love.

I watched as Derek sweated through our awkward first conversation, and yet he was so polite. I wasn't quite sure he even knew who I was, but in the end, that didn't matter. All that mattered was whether he could dance, because if he couldn't, we were in big trouble.

Well, let me tell you something: That kid can dance. I mean, breathtaking, way-beyond-his-years dance. He can also choreograph and teach like nobody's business. His younger sister, Julianne, was already a beloved pro on the show, and as soon as he walked out on that stage, Derek became a fan favorite, too. I knew I was in very good, albeit extremely young hands.

There is no messing around with *DWTS*. After that "at home" meeting, where they got some footage of Derek and me meeting for the first time, and some material to use in promos, we began practicing pretty much right away, holing ourselves up in a dance studio in North Hollywood, where Derek did his best to teach me the cha-cha.

I'd say there is no better way to lose the last of your pregnancy pudge than by doing the cha-cha (or the mambo, or the quickstep, or the fox-trot—you name it) for eight hours a day. I thought chasing after three girls and keeping the laundry going and the meals coming was the most exhausting thing any woman could do, but I was wrong: Training in ballroom dance with enough intensity and rigor so that you can actually do it on live television just a few short weeks after your first lesson is way more exhausting than being home with three kids. Because, after all, you still go home, after practicing all day, and put that mommy hat right back on.

As you know, I'm a dedicated people pleaser, and I wanted to please Derek and be a very good student—I really did. But even he, a soft-spoken, seriously gifted guy, would throw up his hands when, after my forty-eighth attempt at getting a step sequence down, I'd still mess up. From time to time, not wanting to lose his cool, Derek would step away, and I'd flop over in relief, grateful that I had the chance to catch my breath for a moment.

I don't think I've ever sweated so much in my life.

But before I felt anywhere near comfortable with the cha-cha, it was showtime!

Let me tell you about prepping for the big night. First, there was

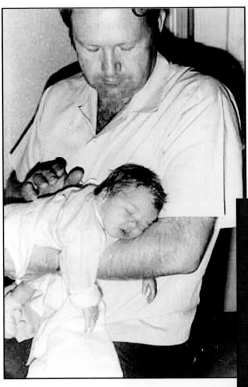

My favorite place:
in my dad's arms.

I loved hanging out in
my Johnny Jump Up.

Already on the move.

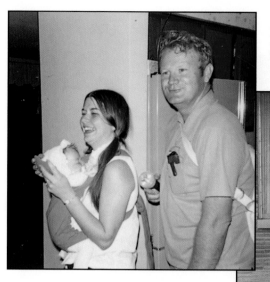

My mom and dad were very
hands-on parents.

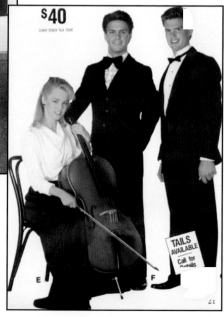

My great-grandfather, who was
a jockey and a barber, let me
shave his head. I still love to
give haircuts.

My mom's family in Illinois. I was never
far away from my mom in those days.

An early modeling gig.

I love family portraits. I already had such an eye for fashion!

I always seemed to have a white dog on my lap.

A different white dog.

With Shannen and Tori at the
People's Choice Awards, 1992.

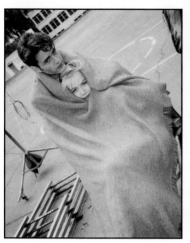

My first job with Jason Priestley
on the set of *Teen Angel*. We were
such babies!

Group shot for the first season of *Beverly Hills 90210*. The show runners gave us *90210* letterman jackets as holiday gifts. Another year they gave us all bicycles!

The full cast.

At the Golden Globes with Tori Spelling and Brian Austin Green, and on the arm of my first husband, 1992.

Luke and me on the set of *Beverly Hills 90210.*

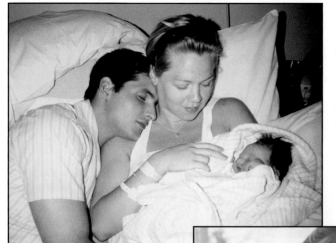

Just after Luca Bella was born. Peter had traveled through the night to meet his new baby. I'm not sure which of us was more tired.

Can't tell which one of us is the baby in this picture.

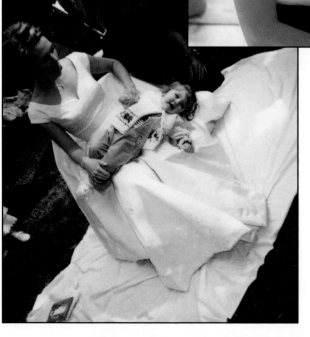

One of my many wedding dresses. I think this was when Kelly left Brandon at the altar. As always, I still had time to play with my baby. That is little Luca Bella on my lap.

Luca Bella at age four.
Sweetest flower girl ever!

Pregnant with Lola Ray. That's Luca....
She wanted to have a baby, too.

This was our "Queen's wedding party."

Baby Number Two: Lola Ray.

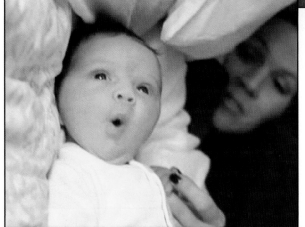

My favorite place to be: snuggling with one of my babies.

Amanda Bynes and me sharing our very special birth date on the set of *What I Like About You*.

Halloween 2003: On the set of *What I Like About You* with baby Lola Ray.

Randy, Adele, Peter and me on the set of the movie where Peter and I met.

Me with a very young Mr. Showbiz and my BFF/assistant, Adele, on the set of *On the Plain Road* in Utah.

My Dad and I loved to go trail riding together. I think I had to hoist him up on that horse.

This is the dress I fell in while on season five of *Dancing with the Stars*.

With my sweet, *young* dance partner, Derek Hough, backstage at *Dancing with the Stars*.

Single mom family time rafting in Colorado, summer 2013.

One of our many RV adventures. I love those trips.

Me and my girls.

Girls' night out at a movie premiere, 2012.

Luca Bella and me shooting *A Little Bit Country* at our ranch in central California.

RVing with Pappy (my dad).

That's me driving a forty-foot RV.

My dad and me on our birthday. He always said I was the best birthday present he ever got.

That's little Lizzey!

That's Pearl, hard at work at LAX.

With my dogs, keeping the
tradition of white pups going.

Me and my mom on
Mothers' Day, 2012.

Mr. and Mrs. Showbiz.

Me and my sis Cammie.

Adele and me in Williamsburg, Brooklyn, 2013.

With Jason and Luke on the set of our Old Navy commercial.

Celebrating my fortieth birthday with friends and family, including my gorgeous girls, Luca Bella, Lola Ray, and Fiona Eve.

the custom-made blue sparkly dress that had cutouts that cleverly hid the parts of my new-mommy body that still needed to be kept under wraps. Derek would be wearing a matching blue jumpsuit, the kind of thing Evel Knievel wore when he was going to, say, try to ride his motorcycle across the Grand Canyon. Now, I don't usually like men in tight spandex, especially anything with rhinestones on it, but I have to say, Derek looked pretty all right in his very tight costume. I guess, for both of us, the producers had the goal of achieving maximum "hotness" without there being any chance of an embarrassing wardrobe malfunction while we danced our butts off.

Once the costume was fitted, it was time for the spray tan. Sweet baby Jesus, the *DWTS* spray tan. I was a spray-tan virgin at this point in my life, and I was damn proud of this fact. So when I was asked to strip and stand in front of a woman wearing construction goggles and holding a hose who looked like she meant business in the worst possible way, I knew this would not be good.

Now, to the producers' credit, the spray tan wasn't mandatory. What I was told was that if I didn't get one, I'd stand out like a giant, very white thumb, and we wouldn't want that, would we? No. We would not.

So there I was, buck naked, in front of a very nice lady who sprayed every last nook and cranny, even ones I didn't know I had. It was an extraordinarily intimate experience, especially the part when she told me to turn around and bend over. It was important, she said while I complied, that there were no visible creases around my butt when I was performing. The things you learn . . . "And it's very nice to meet you, too."

I finally emerged from the spray-tan area a few hours later, a custom-blended shade of dark orange. I was then taken to makeup, where about eight pounds of stage makeup was spackled to my face; then came the false eyelashes, which were painstakingly applied in such a way that I actually thought my eyeballs would dry up and fall out, or that I'd be permanently blinded when the makeup artist was finished.

I staggered out of the makeup room, squeezed into my costume, put on my dancing shoes, and then nearly fell over when they announced the order of appearance.

Guess who had to dance first.

Gulp. Me. Never mind that I looked like a showgirl who had run off and joined the circus. Derek and I heard our names being called by that announcer with the very strange, vaguely Eastern European accent: "Here to dance the cha-cha . . ." Next thing you know, Derek and I were onstage, the lights were blinding, the music was blaring, the crowd was clapping, and we danced our little blond hearts out. Several times, I almost slipped in the puddles of spray tan that were forming all over the stage (I probably lost at least a pound in perspiration, another in anxiety), yet somehow or other, we managed to finish our routine and then found ourselves completely out of breath and standing in front of Carrie, Len, and Bruno, the esteemed and hilariously serious judges of *DWTS*. I don't think I heard a word they said, I was so traumatized and exhausted. But I do know that out of a possible thirty points, we scored a respectable twenty-one.

Done and done. Look who's dancing now.

It felt like before my week-one spray tan had even dried, week two rolled around. I was feeling a little bit better having made it through week one without falling or screwing up in some major way. Going into week two of *DWTS*, I knew I needed to dig in and find a little bit more confidence so we could score a little higher. The dance for week two was the quickstep, a classic ballroom dance—and I felt way more at ease with this style than I had with the cha-cha. I could do this. Right?

All I had to do was get over feeling like I was dancing with a child. Poor Derek. During rehearsal, he begged me to think of him as a man's man—George Clooney, actually—rather than as a boy from Utah. So

I'd look him in the eye, think, *Hi, George*, imagining my voice deep and throaty and . . . then I'd burst out laughing. I didn't mean to be cruel, but, man . . . he was so young!

This was going to be a huge night for me, because my dad, who was pretty incapacitated by this point, and was using a wheelchair to get around, was coming to watch me perform. I knew he'd have a front-row seat, and this made me feel both excited and even more crazy nervous.

At least this time, we didn't have to dance first, so I had the chance to go through a few rounds of hyperventilating backstage until . . .

We were on!

Man, we were killing it! I was gliding around the stage, dressed in a flowing pastel-pink number, while Derek looked dashing in a black tux. KT Tunstall's hit "Suddenly I See" was our song, and I was thinking, *Check this out. . . . Suddenly I'm dancing. . . .* I knew I had to bring more confidence to my game that night, and so I locked eyes with Derek, straightened my back (the judges had commented on my lack of proper dance posture the week before), and decided to just trust that we wouldn't mess up. And we didn't, until . . .

As it happened, we were finishing our number *right in front of my father*, and the music swelled as we were moving into our superflashy last move, in which I'd slide down onto the floor, glide between Derek's legs, and he'd twirl elegantly above me and then, ta-da! *Fini!* But when he released me down to the floor, I felt this weird tug on my dress, and the next thing I knew, Derek was kind of falling over me, his shoe stuck in the fabric of my gown. He's so good at what he does that he recovered, but it had happened. There I was, on my ass. The first fall of the season. Oops.

We finished up and made our way over to the judges' table, where Bruno, God bless him, blurted out, "It was like Leo and Kate in *Titanic*!" After that remark, I didn't hear a word, just a loud buzzing in my head. It was the buzz of shame. I felt really bad, because my husband and kids—and my dad—were all there. In the end, we must have done something right, though, because we still managed to pull off a score of three sevens, for another twenty-one. What a relief! Because after all the niceties and hoopla of the opening two weeks, where we were all treated with kid gloves, as behooves big "stars" like us, now the gloves were off. It was time to kick some serious ass—this was a highly competitive thing, you know? I mean, more than twenty million—twenty *million*—people were watching from home and texting or calling in and deciding our fate (which could be shockingly at odds with our judges' scores). And this was the first week someone would be eliminated. When it came time to announce who was out, I just held my breath as Tom Bergeron asked actress Josie Maran to say her good-byes. Oh. My. God. It was kind of horrifying to watch, and it made me determined to hang on as long as I possibly could. Otherwise that buzz of shame would follow me home and dog me for the rest of my days—or so I stupidly thought.

I was in with a crazy, fierce mix of pros, some of whom had danced before (Mel B from the Spice Girls and Sabrina Bryan, a Cheetah Girl) but the people you really had to watch your back with were the ones with the serious stage experience, those ageless and indefatigable creatures who had been onstage with a mike in hand since before I was born. Yup. I'm talking Wayne Newton and Marie Osmond, in particular.

Wayne, a total doll of a man, had the whole Vegas, easy-swagger, "I've got the whole audience in the palm of my hand" thing down pat. I mean, he'd practically invented it. He also happened to be born on April 3, so he was my birthday twin, which created an extraspecial bond between us, too. Never mind that the man couldn't touch his toes—he was having the time of his life, and he knew how to make sure everyone around him was, too. He and his wife are the loveliest people, and I felt very honored to get to know them both. I adore them.

Then there is Marie Osmond. Wow. What I can I say? She had the whole crazy, giant doll-collecting world behind her, not to mention the

Church of Jesus Christ of Latter-day Saints, the state of Utah, and what? Like five hundred brothers and their legions of utterly devoted fans? I mean, her fan base was huge. Giant. Colossal. We all understood pretty early on that Marie was going to be the juggernaut, the person we'd all be chasing, and with each passing week she was proving us right—even the night she fainted onstage, which only seemed to kindle her determination, and which galvanized her awesomeness in the eyes of her vast audience, and us, her fellow competitors; I mean, who passes out on live TV and then, five minutes later, cracks jokes about it?

Then there were the athletes, who were quiet but so focused it was intimidating. Even scarier was how freaking graceful these guys were. I'm talking about the boxer Floyd Mayweather Jr. and the Indy race car driver Hélio Castroneves, who elegantly and stealthily kicked all of our asses—and Hélio then won the whole damn thing. He was incredible: consistent, professional, a delight to watch. And so was his partner, Julianne, who just happened to be my baby partner's baby sister.

I won't bore you with the blow-by-blow of each week, but let's just say that I surprised myself, and week after week I'd make the cut. At home, I was becoming something of a legend. I mean, can you think of anything more awesome to do as the mom of three girls than be on *Dancing with the Stars*? I was getting seriously buff, too. I lost around ten pounds, but my shape was completely rearranged by all that dancing in pretty phenomenal ways—inches came off, the butt was sky-high, the boobs. It was pretty amazing! Peter was blown away, too, because he knew how freaked out I was by crowds and being in public, and I could tell that with each passing week, even he was surprised by how well I was doing. In a word, I was killing it. And it felt good.

In the end, I made it all the way to the semifinals, even picking up a few perfect scores of thirty on my way to a very respectable fourth-place finish.

HOLIDAYS AND HOSPITALS

Why is it that the highest highs are always followed by the lowest lows? Is this what they mean by Murphy's Law? And who the hell was Murphy, anyway?

Dancing with the Stars wrapped just before Thanksgiving, which was a beautiful, beautiful thing: I missed being at home with my girls, of course, but I also couldn't wait to eat whatever I wanted again, knowing that I wasn't going to be sewn into a skimpy dance costume come Monday, or whatever day of the week it was when we danced "live."

We celebrated my having cleared the dancing hurdle by taking the girls for a quick island getaway. It was just what my tired muscles and beat-up feet needed: sun, sand, and a lot of nothing else.

When we got home, we put together a big family Thanksgiving celebration, but my middle daughter, Lola, came down with something and . . . she just couldn't shake it. My normally upright and helpful, superloving five-year-old was curled up in a quiet ball, achy and under the weather.

At first we figured she'd just brought home the big, gnarly school virus that takes out a bunch of kids right before a holiday break. (This is definitely Murphy's Law, right?) But almost right away, I knew that whatever was going on with Lola was not something run-of-the-mill. Lola, who had the sweet energy of a frisky little colt, was now as limp as a noodle, and so depleted that she barely spoke. Seeing her so sick pressed my mama-bear panic button, and we mobilized around her immediately.

The first call we made was to her pediatrician, and she expressed concern right out of the gate, with little Lola's body covered in red hive-like bumps, and a fever that seemed to stick around the scary hundred-and-five-degree range. Clearly this was not a typical bacterial infection, because the drugs they'd prescribed for her weren't touching it. But what did we know? We followed the doctor's advice and gave the treatment a few days, and pretty rapidly, things for Lola went from bad to worse: In no time at all, she was suffering such severe joint pain that she couldn't even walk. When she could no longer make it to the bathroom, we knew we were in serious trouble, and so we whisked her to the hospital.

Let me tell you, people: You do not want your daughter (or son) admitted to a major medical center if no one has a clue as to what is ailing your child, and even just thinking about what that meant for poor Lola, all these years later, well, it still ignites a firestorm of maternal rage in me.

Here we were, in the great city of Los Angeles, the land of Hollywood and, we thought, state-of-the-art hospitals, with a very, very sick child on our hands. Because of her overt symptoms (high fever, bright body rash, severe aches and pains), her team of doctors immediately jumped on a diagnosis of scarlet fever and began to pump her full of more antibiotics. When her symptoms worsened, they moved on to subjecting her to a vast and fruitless array of painful and invasive tests, including (but not limited to) testing for leukemia, performing a bone-marrow biopsy, and taking out a lymph node and biopsying that, too. Every day they were poking her with needles and ratcheting up the testing, and every day Lola was getting worse.

Peter and I were beside ourselves. Here we were, pacing the halls of the hospital, waiting to hear whether our daughter would test positive for a terrifying cancer or some other horrible disease that very well might take her life. To describe this time as harrowing is an understatement, and I get traumatized all over again just thinking about having to step out of Lola's room—after she'd been bruised by more needles than I could count and she'd cried herself hoarse—in order to not completely lose it in front of her. I remember once having to run out of her room, and I was so overwhelmed with pity for her, and fear for her, that I just dropped to my knees, unable to breathe or speak, sobbing uncontrollably.

Nothing is worse than your child being so sick.

While the doctors fumbled along, Peter and I were constantly on the computer, doing research like mad, determined to do what all the experts around us could not, which was to figure out what sinister bacteria or virus had invaded our daughter and then find out how to kill it once and for all.

I had a theory, of course, as all moms do when their child gets sick, but the white lab coats didn't want to hear it. We'd been on that tropical vacation, and Lola had gotten her hair braided on the beach, and the braids had been capped off by tinfoil. The tin paper on one of the braids had cut into her neck, and the next thing you know, we were home and she was perilously ill. To this day, I'm convinced that some strange, tropical disease made its way into her via that big wound that bloomed around that cut on the side of her neck, that this was indeed the point of infection. But of course the world-famous infectious-disease specialists who were brought in didn't see it that way, and so they fumbled on.

This craziness went on for nine days—*nine days*. It went on until Lola reached the breaking point and she became downright hostile and noncompliant, and so, frankly, untreatable. Here she was, five years old, unable to sleep or rest at all because she would panic and freak out every time anyone opened the door of her hospital room, fearing she would be stuck with a giant needle, or be forced to give more blood, or be hooked up to some scary-looking machine. And who could blame her? After a week and a half, the geniuses who were looking after her were no closer to a diagnosis, and our little girl was not getting any better.

So we made the decision to bring her home. It was Christmastime, and we would be damned if our baby was going to spend the holidays sick and in a hospital, surrounded by people who just didn't seem to give a shit about her. Instead, we found a doctor who specializes in juvenile rheumatoid arthritis, and he immediately and correctly diagnosed Lola with Still's disease. Her treatment began immediately, and the new doctor put her on the right combination of steroids and anti-inflammatory agents so that the acute episode she was suffering (which typically lasts for a couple of months) could run its course.

Thank God we did this. Still's is an extremely rare disease (it affects only one in a million people, mostly children), and if it's not treated aggressively and early, there can be all sorts of long-term damage to a child's joints and internal organs. No one knows for sure what causes it, but research does point to an invasive microbe as the likely culprit, something, say, that you might pick up on a tropical island. Other theories are that it is an autoimmune disease that can, if not treated early and properly, become chronic. In the end, the way of it doesn't matter, because Lola—all of us—lucked out: She suffered a terrible, acute case of Still's, but she's one of the lucky few who, thank God, recovered completely.

Now if only I were so lucky.

RACING THE CLOCK

We rolled into the New Year of 2008 with things looking up in our household: Lola was feeling better and the girls were all thriving in school. But things up at the ranch weren't going so well. My dad was really deteriorating and was receiving dialysis now. My sister Wendy and my mom were with him 'round the clock and taking really good, loving care of him, but he needed nursing assistance now, too. I was bouncing between the ranch and home in LA, trying to be there for everybody.

We always did something fun with the girls for their spring break, and this year would be no exception. LEGOLAND, down near San Diego, was the draw, and while Peter and the girls excitedly planned our trip, I couldn't shake the feeling that maybe this year, we ought to just stay home.

As winter turned into spring, my dad's health really hit the skids. He suffered a serious bout of congestive heart failure and wound up in the hospital over Easter. His blood pressure was so dangerously low that he was in a kind of woozy state that left him weakened and rambling.

Between all that, and the now daily dialysis, I just didn't want to leave him. But I also didn't want to let the kids and Peter down.

What to do?

I decided to stay the course and go south with my family. Before we packed up and left for San Diego, I came up to Santa Barbara, where my dad was hospitalized, to give him a hug and bring him some treats. My dad loved candy, and he always got a kick out of it when I'd smuggle some into the hospital for him. But not this time. Instead, when I handed him a Snickers bar, his favorite, he shook his head and said, "Nuts equal losers." I laughed and asked what he meant and he said he didn't want the nurses to see him with nuts in his teeth. This struck me as incredibly sad and I didn't know what to say, so I just kissed him and left the candy bar on his bedside table.

My mom was there, too, and I hugged her close. She'd taken such good care of my father all those years; in fact, she had kept him alive by keeping track of all of his medications and advocating hard for him when his doctors weren't communicating with one another, or when they weren't listening to what he or my mother said. She really had loved him through sickness and in health, and this is something I will always admire about her.

Before I left that day, I did what I always did: I filled his water glass, kissed him, and then I made sure he was all tucked in, the thin, ugly green hospital blankets tucked neat and comfy around him. I took extra care arranging them around his feet, which were long and skinny and stuck straight up to the skies. Then I gently squeezed his toes, which was my way of saying, "Love you, Dad!" Before I left, I stopped at the door, looked him right in the eyes, and said, "I'll see you when I get back; you'll be here, right?" He knew I was scared. "I'll be here" was what he said. But the look in his eyes told me that he was scared, too.

I went back down to LA and we packed up and headed south for our LEGOLAND vacation. We checked into our hotel, had a great night together, and then we went to bed. But when I woke up that first morning on vacation, I was achy and feverish and felt like I had the flu. I just couldn't find the energy to get up and play, so Peter took the girls off to the beach so I could rest. I slept almost all day, and when I woke late in the afternoon, I checked in with my mom. She'd made my dad his favorite steak dinner and had brought it into the hospital. He'd loved it, she said. I went to bed that night feeling better and less nervous about my dad's status.

Before the sun rose, the phone rang. I sat bolt upright, knowing in my bones that this was the call I'd been dreading all my life. It was my mom. Dad was very sick again and he was asking for me. I could hear what sounded like a struggle, and I asked my mother what was going on. "It's your father. He wants to talk to you, but he's not making any sense, honey," she said. There was more rustling and then my dad was on the phone, but whatever he was saying was unintelligible. I tried to make out the garbled words and it sounded like he was saying something about my girls and protecting them. Then my mom took the phone back and said quietly that she was sure the time was near and that I should come back as soon as possible.

I woke Peter, and before I knew it I was having a full-blown panic attack. How would I get to my dad? We were two hundred miles away, which meant about a four-hour drive. While I paced around, crying, Peter tracked down a rental car, and within an hour I had kissed him and the girls good-bye and sped off. I was crying so hard that I could hardly see, so I just followed the signs that said, "North."

I drove as fast as I could in those dark hours, and I stopped only once, to pee. I wish now that I hadn't. I managed to make it to Santa Barbara in about three hours, and I pulled into the hospital parking lot and just parked and ran. I flew through the automatic doors and ran to an elevator, and jumped on just as the doors were closing. There was only one other person in that elevator, and it was my sister Wendy. There I was, sweaty and panting, and there was Wendy, looking down at the floor, not talking. I tried to catch my breath, and when the elevator opened, I looked at Wendy and then ran. But I was stopped outside the door to my dad's room by a strange man and woman—and my mom. "Where's Dad?" I blurted out. My mom said, "These people wanted to talk to you in that room over there first," and she gently turned me toward an open door. "Okay. Let's go!" I said, and I was led into a tiny room, asked to take a seat, and then my mom and Wendy crowded into the room with us. Then the strange woman shut the door and everyone just stared at me, except Wendy, who stared at the floor. Then they told me my dad was dead. I had missed him by twelve minutes.

My body convulsed and coiled up. I sprang up from that chair like a wild animal. Sounds came up from somewhere inside me that rattled everyone, including me, and those two strangers tried to hold on to me, but that just caused me to fly to the door and bolt from that shitty little room. I tore down the hall and instinctively found the room where my father's body was. There he was, under that same disgusting green blanket, and I noticed his feet were all wrong: One was still pointing up, but the other had fallen over sideways. That was when I lost it completely. I threw myself across my dad's solid body and clung to him, just like I had as a child. It was the place where I felt the safest, the place I had always yearned for, the place I long for as I write this now. I was wailing and I couldn't stop. I didn't stop until, after a long while, the nurses came and gave me a powerful sedative.

I woke up later in his bed, up at the ranch, in a horrible, horrible haze. My friend Ed was there with me, sitting on the edge of the bed, holding my hand. He didn't say much; he just cried with me and then left me to sleep. I wanted to sleep forever.

Something shifted then for me. Some place of mistrust and distrust broke open and it caused me to turn inward, to close myself off—even from the people I loved best.

This, I was to learn, is what grief can do.

A LITTLE BIT . . . DEVASTATED

A couple of years ago, on the cusp of turning forty, I found myself feeling—despite being knee-deep in raising my kids, and fully immersed in what I thought was a pretty solid, normal-ups-and-downs kind of marriage—alone in ways that really confused me. I mean, I was married to a man I loved, and together we had built a beautiful family. I was able to be at home with our three beautiful daughters, yet still able to work when I felt I wanted or needed to. My life—by any reasonable measure—was blessed and rich beyond belief. I had financial security, a beautiful home in LA, a ranch up in the Santa Ynez Valley. In other words, I had it all. And I felt like I had it all. But I couldn't shake the feeling of being alone in the midst of all of that bounty. I still wasn't able to break out of the shock of losing my father. There I was, walking, talking, and living my day-to-day life, but what I wasn't doing was feeling. I was shut down and locked out of my own life. Trapped in a bubble, with everything and everyone around me at arm's length. At least, that was how it felt. And I didn't know what to do about it.

My husband was away a lot then, working across the country on location on a film project that he'd written, was producing, and was starring in. I was thrilled for him that he was taking his career to the next level, but I was also, I can see now, feeling a bit resentful and itchy in ways that I couldn't quite identify. I wanted something, needed something, but I had no way of accessing what that was, of finding a way to articulate what had me pinned down. I needed to reach out—badly—but because I had no idea what I needed to ask for, I did the opposite.

All I know is that I felt like I was *waiting*: waiting for him to come home, waiting for him to be free to join me in the day-to-day of our family life, waiting for the next job to be lined up that would take him far away from us again. I was always waiting for . . . something that I didn't want to happen.

And in a weird way, by waiting for it, I was making space for it.

Something was shifting. The ground beneath me was beginning to crack and crumble so imperceptibly that I just didn't know it was happening. But like an animal that senses a thunderstorm on the breeze, I intuitively knew that I needed to duck and take cover.

I packed up my kids and moved us up to the ranch, telling myself this was the chance, while they were still very young, to have them live out of the city and close to their grandma. I thought it would allow them to experience a simpler kind of life, like the one I'd had when I was a kid, one without all the hustle and distractions that are LA. At the ranch, they'd be able to ride horses, feed the chickens, and live in a town where everybody smiled and waved, rather than flipping you the bird or throwing water bottles at your car when you accidentally pulled out in front of them. It would be good for them, I thought, and it would be good for me, too. We'd simply relocate our small tribe and spend some serious quality time with one another. I thought that being up at the ranch would give me the space I needed to wrangle this awful restlessness to the ground.

But of course this wasn't the full truth. Peter and I had been struggling for some time, and I didn't know what to do but take myself out of the situation. I was angry, I was hurt, but I didn't know at what, exactly. All I knew was that I was being consumed by pain and I had no idea how to connect with him without all of the pent-up wounds muddling my efforts. It was frustrating. And crushing, and I honestly believed that if I had some space—if we had some space—things would sort themselves out.

Peter agreed to this, mostly, I think, because he wanted me to be happy, and he felt that if this would bring me back to myself, then perhaps we would be able to heal our relationship. We had, during the course of our marriage, talked about building our own place up there, so we went ahead and bought another fifteen acres up in the Valley (as the Santa Ynez Valley is known by locals) and we decided that we'd build an eco-friendly family ranch on it. We had ambitious building plans drawn up, and then we thought, Why don't we create a show around building our "green" dream home? Peter began working on a pitch and sent it out to the networks. In no time at all, the Country Music Television network (CMT) scooped it up.

But then it happened.

The ground that had been cracking and shifting finally split open and pretty much swallowed me whole: Peter came home, and told me that he didn't think he wanted to be married to me any longer, and he thought it best that we separate so that we could get a better sense of where we stood with each other.

This was not something I consciously expected; in fact, I'd say that I didn't even allow myself to entertain the idea that my husband may have reached the end of his rope, too. I understand, now, how frustrated he was at how unreachable I'd become, but at the time, conceding that we'd reached a possibly unbridgeable break in our marriage was not something I was prepared for, psychologically or emotionally. I was still in the fugue state brought on by the loss of my father, and though I knew it was my responsibility to figure out how to break through it, I just hadn't been able to. Now, with this news, I was nearly undone.

We had been together, then, for seventeen years. Of course, our life together had not been perfect: Being married is hard; being young parents is harder. Being married to an actor (for both of us) is even harder still. We'd certainly spent our fair share of time on the couches of therapists during our nearly two decades together, but for me, dealing with the problems but having the secure feeling that we were in it together was what made it work and what made it worthwhile. As long as we were both in there, thrashing through things, it was going to work out. Whenever we figured out how to push ourselves up and over an impasse, whenever one or the other of us relented just enough for there to be some breathing room, we'd find ourselves in a better place. But for some time now, I had not been able to do that heavy lifting. I wasn't up for thrashing through anything. I had become a shadow of myself and, without feeling like I had any control over it, I had been fading farther and farther away from him. And now Peter was no longer up for the fight, either. But how do you fight with someone who has become a ghost of herself? I wanted things to be different. I wanted to be different. But here we were. I was devastated by the news that he was no longer in love with me.

In the midst of this marital crisis, we had CMT to contend with. We had signed a contract with them, and rather than our just canceling it outright, somehow or other the project morphed into being about me, a mom on her own with her three daughters on a working ranch.

I was in a complete haze with no sense of which way was up, no facility to make any kind of life decision, so I turned to Mr. Showbiz and asked what he thought we ought to do.

"Maybe it's a good idea. It will keep you busy. Keep you distracted. Keep you grounded while you figure all this out."

Before you get any suspicious ideas about Mr. Showbiz's intentions, let me just say that he was as stunned as I was by this turn of events; he was so fond of both Peter and me, and he knew me well enough to know that this loss could really do me in, so his intentions in this regard were only good. He was—we all were—scrambling to figure out how to keep things afloat, to keep me from completely going under the waves, and this show was the life ring that was closest at hand.

Mr. Showbiz knows me well, and so he understood that the show must go on. I did what I tend to do when I don't know what I should do: I defaulted into my people-pleaser mode and became the "trouper," the pro, and I said okay.

As hard as it is to believe—for both you and me—I agreed to have the first days of my life after having been left by my husband filmed for a television show. This was not, I must say, the best decision I've made. But at the time, I just couldn't even muster the strength to say no.

In truth, I knew next to nothing about the mechanics of making a reality television show. The upshot is that you have strange people in your life—and by in your life I mean in your bathroom, in your bedroom (for real), and in every nook and cranny of your private space for days and weeks on end. It's not, on the face of it, the most therapeutic kind of project to take on, but we will eventually get to all of that.

Agreeing to do the show meant that I would have to process all of this (and, as you know by now, I'm not always the quickest to react or recover) in front of a film crew first, and then in front of a pretty big TV audience. I'd forgotten that I don't really possess the ability to hide my emotions or even edit them before they come bursting forth. In other words, though I'm a pretty good actress, I am, in my private life, straightforward—even, some would say, to a fault; I'm not one to bull-shit, not one to pull any punches. There would be no hiding behind a character this time: It would be me at my lowest.

So much for getting away from it all so I could I lick my wounds privately while trying to pick up the pieces of my shattered heart and patch them back together.

But there was an upside, a silver lining of sorts. Reality TV (if you still believe in the "realness" of reality TV, please skip over this next part, or better yet, read it and learn the truth) is just contrived enough so that there is a bit of a barrier between your "real" life and the one that is portrayed on the show. It's a tiny margin, but it was there, and I was to learn, mercifully, that it's just big enough so that I could actually make the show without totally losing it on camera. This was the upside.

So I found myself moving into production on a show about my life, a life that lay broken at my feet. I had no idea how this would work out, how we would fare, but we—I—had made a commitment and I was going to honor it.

So let the cameras roll.

IT'S NOT EXACTLY THE OK CORRAL

I probably should have consulted with Mr. Showbiz before I spill some of the trade secrets of reality television production, but I didn't—so here goes. Contrary to what some of you may think, reality television isn't entirely unscripted. For each episode, there's a basic story arc that's set up in advance, and though there's no written script, everyone knows what the basic narrative is for that episode, and so everyone sets up and the cameras start rolling and then . . . the best improvised moments that are caught on film are the ones that are edited into that day's story. Well, that's the goal, anyway.

In the case of my show, which was called *A Little Bit Country*, the producers brought in a character who would serve as my foil. This was Corrine, who was brought on board to work as my new personal assistant and to give me another adult to interact with.

As my comedic foil and partner on the show, poor Corrine had to do all kinds of things that no person in his or her right mind should ever agree to do. But she did, often, and we can chalk it up to taking one for the team.

In one episode, we went to a local livestock auction to buy a cow, and while we were waiting for the bidding to start, Corinne happened to mention that it was her understanding that someone who is about to milk a cow actually sucks that cow's teat, in order to get the milk flowing. This was not made up or written for the show: She actually believed this. Of course, this was the most absurd thing I'd ever heard, but Corinne would not let it go. So I made a bet with her: How about if we polled a few of the local cowboys and ranchers sitting around us to find out if this was true or not? If she was wrong, she'd have to suck a cow's teat. If I was wrong, I'd have to do the same. Corinne, God bless her, made the bet. I will end this story by saying simply that I won this particular bet, and once we'd bought our cow and gotten her home, the cameras rolled while Corinne paid up. This was not pretty. But you know what? Mr. Showbiz was right: This kind of thing *was* distracting. And I needed that. My girls needed it. We needed some levity and some life and some sense of purpose and camaraderie around the place to lift our spirits.

I took advantage of the work of the ranch (we had horses, a cow for a second, the pig, goats, lots of dogs, chickens, and cats) and the work of mothering my little girls, and, of course, the work of the show, to keep the deep sorrow I felt at bay. Until finally I just couldn't anymore. It happened one day when I least expected it. While Corrine and I were walking toward the house, she blurted out, "So where is your husband?" I was so unprepared for this that I froze, and then, after an awkward silence, I told her the truth. I managed to gulp in some air and stammer, "We . . . are separated." At that point, the well opened up, and I barely managed to hold it together for the rest of the shooting day.

Now, the show was no longer just a light comedy about two women and three girls navigating life on a ranch. The "real" part of this production was that I was recently separated and now all the world (or those who tuned in) would know. In other words, the revolution, or, in my case, the devastation, was being televised. Doesn't that sound like great TV?

Here's the deal: I had promised myself, for those intense but short weeks while we filmed the show, that I'd be in on the "gag," that I'd go along with the premise that I was a city slicker trying out the country thing—a contemporary take on *Green Acres*, if you will. I was supposed to play the straight man to my "assistant" Corinne's fish-out-of-water shtick, and I didn't anticipate being asked this kind of question. But now that the cat was out of the bag, there would be no more acting for me, no more pretending, at least not about the reality of my marital status. And this caused quite a dilemma for me professionally, because I was so coiled up, so bogged down by so much emotion, that I just didn't know where to put it all. I'd wake up, open my eyes, realize I was on the cusp of this huge, massive life change (my marriage very possibly ending for good), and then I'd step into my kitchen, foggy-headed from the immensity of it all, and there would be about a half dozen people milling around—the camera and sound crew for the show! I'd snap back into the present and realize there was a show happening. Here were these people, all waiting for me to do something funny or spontaneous, and I just wanted to crawl back into my bed and give in to the self-pity and sorrow that wanted to consume me. As good an actress as I can be, I just couldn't be *A Little Bit Country* Jennie and not at the same time be heartbroken, frightened Jennie. It was all just out there.

Ugh.

Now I had done it; I had broken the unspoken Garth/Facinelli family code of silence, big-time.

Learning to be a separated person sucks. To all of you out there who may (and I pray you don't) have to go there, do not—under any circumstances—do so while making a reality TV show.

I guess I thought the best way to handle it all was to be open and honest and real. Which was at the time the only thing I was even re-motely capable of being. But you know what? It is possible to be too real—especially for reality TV: God, I look back at those episodes now and I want to shout at the screen, "Someone kidnap that poor blonde and take her away before she says something. . . . Oh, no! Too late!" It's like watching a train wreck over and over and over again. At least, that was what I thought—until I started to hear from viewers that I had made it easier for them to not feel so alone, so alienated while they went through their own separation, and I felt a bit better. Then I heard from another, and another, and . . .

But this outpouring of support didn't make me feel like it had been a wise move on my part. I mean, I do have three young girls who watched all that then—and can certainly watch it again if they ever want to. I tried to be diplomatic and sensitive to all parties, and sweet Jesus, I tried to keep my stupid tears from flowing for all the world to see, but there just came a point when the floodgates gave. . . .

Along with the fan letters came a ton of flak, too, from all kinds of people who criticized me for talking about my stuff in such an open, raw, and unglamorous way. For a while, I listened to this criticism and felt really bad about myself. It took a long, long time get past the sense of failure that engulfed me when my marriage ended.

I still sometimes wish I could erase that whole time of my life, es-pecially what's caught on that reality show film, but you know what? In the end, I did the best I could; I spoke the truth. My truth. And that's got to count for something. Because at the end of the day, I'm really all I've got, and I'm the one I've got to live with.

Staying on the ranch once the cat was out of the bag just wasn't an option. The show had taken on a new, bizarre direction, and I needed to figure out a way to shift my energy, big-time.

I told the producers we needed a change of scene, and so they sug-gested that I take a weekend, perhaps spend a day or two without having to be in "mommy" mode. They came up with the idea of sending me to a "love retreat" at Esalen, an outrageously beautiful and world-renowned retreat center located on the Pacific Ocean in Big Sur, California. I called Adele, who is now a therapist, and asked her what she thought about this. She did some quick research and thought it couldn't hurt; why not? And she even offered to come with me. So here it was, life ring number two, in the form of a love retreat. I was barely treading water at that point, but when this was pushed toward me I reached out and took it. So, in the middle of filming the show, Adele, Corinne, and I hit the road in search of some healing, some relief. And the show's camera crew hit the road, too.

LOVE ON THE ROCKS

Esalen is quite possibly the most idyllic, beautiful spot of land on the West Coast. It's set on a rocky bluff overlooking the Pacific Ocean, and its grounds are just the right amount of wild and rugged, cut through with serene and easy. It's a place that feels out of time—and that's the whole point. You come to Esalen when you need to let go of your worldly cares and woes and give your weary soul the chance to take a little breather. And I needed that badly.

I'd read a book called *Ten Things to Do When Your Life Falls Apart* by a woman named Daphne Rose Kingma, a relationship and love expert. She would be leading a retreat called "Love After Love," which was a concept I really needed to try to get hold of.

We checked into our rooms, which were kind of no-frills, like a summer camp for grown-ups. The quiet there was intense—even compared to nighttime on the ranch. Our weekend would be spent largely in group sessions, led by Daphne, and because these would be attended by other "civilians," the camera crew that had come along with us wouldn't be allowed to film them. And thank God for that, because for once in my life, I opened up some and shared my feelings in a small group of humans who were, each one of them, utterly present and supportive and attuned and so damn loving.

I was able to talk about how losing my dad, and now Peter—the two most important men in my life—landed a one-two punch that had knocked the wind right out of me. I just hadn't been managing these losses very well, and I realized, in that very caring and easy energy environment at Esalen, that I hadn't had anyone to talk to about these losses. Back at the ranch, I was with my little girls and my mom, and I felt like it was my job to stiff-upper-lip it as best I could.

I was every inch my dad's daughter: stoic, withholding, uncomfortable sharing my feelings. And unfortunately I've perfected acting as if everything is okay, even when it's not. I was an avoider of the highest order, and letting my guard down, letting my feelings actually break through the surface, turned out to be a much-needed and unexpected *relief.*

To say I was sad is an understatement. I had been with Peter for almost twenty years, and I felt anguish at failing in our marriage, at not being able to make it last, not just for our daughters' sake, but for mine.

But I also felt angry. Super-scorching-hot angry: at myself for not being enough for him; at him for not believing I was enough for him. And especially for not knowing how to tell him how I really felt, to ask him for what I needed. It was a revelation, letting all this anger out, because I'd worked so damn hard for so damn long to keep it bottled up and out of sight that it had cost me everything.

I spent some good one-on-one time with Daphne, too, and she let me know that the anger I was feeling was normal and healthy and necessary—as long as I kept expressing it and releasing it, from both my body and my soul.

I cried a lot that weekend. So did Corinne and Adele. I think it was cathartic for all of us to talk about how, at one time or another, love had failed us and how we had failed love. I know it was healing for me, and I walked away from that love retreat feeling something I hadn't felt in a very long time: a glimmer of hope.

It was time for me to go back up to the ranch, wrap up that crazy show, and figure out what I was going to do with the rest of my life.

Ready or not, it was time.

OPA!

was in no mood for a party. I had been living up at the ranch with the girls for nearly two years, but now, with the end of my marriage official, I felt like it was time to get back to civilization and get back to work. Get back to life. But knowing this and actually doing it were two very different things. The fact of the matter was that I was depressed, I was fat, I was tired. I was suffering from shell shock. I was having trouble getting out of bed, never mind mustering the energy required to pack up four people and a bunch of animals for a long-distance move. Especially now that I would be doing it alone. I didn't feel like seeing anyone, I hadn't showered in days, and I'd find myself, in the middle of a chore, suddenly paralyzed by how conflicted I felt about moving back to LA. I was pretty much a walking zombie, and so I just shuffled from room to room, doing the best I could.

The kitchen was the last room to be packed. So on that last full day at the ranch, I got out the bubble wrap and began, for what seemed the thousandth time, to pack up the Williams-Sonoma cream-colored dish-ware, our everyday set of dishes. I had moved so many times—why was this time so freaking hard? I reached for a plate, and just as I was about to lay it on the sheet of bubble wrap in front of me, my hand abruptly stopped as though it were paralyzed, and I watched as the plate just left my fingertips and fell, in what felt like slow motion, to the floor. *Crash!* Just then I heard Liz, my assistant, shout out in her cheery way, "I know! You ought to have a dish-breaking party!" Did she think I'd dropped that plate on purpose? She came around the corner then. "Really. It will make you feel better." She was smiling at me. I looked from Liz to the stack of dishes on the counter. I loved those dishes so much: They were thick and durable and so creamy. And besides, we'd had them forever: I think they may have even been a wedding present. Liz went off to finish what she was doing and I looked down and kicked the broken bits of that plate out of my way. I started to pack again. I picked up another plate and . . . whoops! It, too, hit the floor. I picked up another and again, as if in slow motion, I watched as the small salad plate seemed to do a swan dive out of my hand and land, with a perfect smash, on the wooden floor of my tiny farmhouse kitchen.

It seemed that if I wasn't going to throw myself a plate-breaking party, the universe was going to do it for me. There I was, in my sweat-pants (which I'd probably slept in), no makeup, my hair a mess, my feet surrounded by broken bits of dishes. I realized I felt better. So I picked up a teacup. *Crash!* Then a bowl. *Smash!* Then another bowl, and a plate, and a saucer, and . . . what was this? A full setting for ten? I lost myself in a frenzy of dish dropping. I was not cursing and hurling those lovely plates. I was simply letting them slide out of my hand, letting gravity do its job. It was awesome! In no time at all, the whole cupboard full of dishes was now a pretty good sea of shards, and I was standing in the middle of it. I was sweaty and a little shaky from the adrenaline rush this gave me, and I felt a little disoriented. But I also felt better. Lighter.

After all that crashing of pottery, I stood, panting, and noticed the house was absolutely still and quiet. Liz had used her incredible sixth sense and had coaxed everyone—including the movers—out of the house so that I could have some space.

Looking down at all that broken pottery was like looking into a crystal ball; I felt as if it were trying to tell me something I badly needed to hear, that there was some wisdom in all that wreckage. But no profound insight was coming to me, just the acknowledgment that there was a heap of broken stuff there. Broken like I had been.

I got the broom and swept up the mess. *Well*, I thought. *There's one less box I have to unpack back in LA.* After that, I was able to get on with my work, and I finished packing up the kitchen, and that night I took a long, hot shower, and ate something healthful, and slept better than I had in months. I was, bit by bit, beginning to lighten my load.

When I go up to the ranch now, I like to see the gashes from that impromptu dish-breaking party in that wooden floor. I can't imagine fixing it, because then I'd be erasing an important part of my history. "Something happened here" is what those marks say to me. Some living went on. Maybe there was even a party. *Opa!*

Thanks, Liz.

A NEW DAY, A NEW HOODIE

Coming back to LA was almost as stressful as filming that reality show. That's because the tabloid media had decided that the failure of my marriage was big news. Being hounded by the paparazzi was the last thing I needed.

There's this really ridiculous line of thinking that goes something like this: Once you become famous, you give up your right to privacy. That by your choosing to be an actor, your life becomes public domain. I don't think my fans feel this way at all, but all the hacks and hounds who make their living by feeding the insatiable gossip beast certainly do.

I don't think I'm alone in saying that this is the biggest load of bullshit that those of us who work in Hollywood have to put up with. But because of the way our laws work, and because I try, you know, to be a civilized human being, the whole paparazzi game is something that, for the most part, I've learned to tolerate. I've been at this a long time, and so I've honed my ability to compartmentalize my feelings about the paparazzi. When I'm angry or my righteous indignation flares up, I practice a kind of paparazzi Zen, wherein I set my face in "neutral" and I just put every ounce of my focus into breathing or walking or, now, staring at my cell phone. It's important to do this when you're being stalked by a camera, because if you don't, you can pretty much guarantee that the most spectacularly hideous picture of you of all time will wind up on the cover of some rag the very next day. But since there's not a whole hell of a lot you—or anyone—can do about this, you have no choice but to figure out how to coexist with all the unwelcome cameras.

Looking back, way back to those faraway days when I first started out in the business, I realize how lucky we were that we came of age, we *90210*ers, before there even was such a thing as the Internet. There were no smart phones with their fancy cameras, no Twitter, or TMZ, or Instagram, or any of these new "social" technologies that make it possible to take a photo of anyone, anywhere, anytime.

In the olden days, meaning twenty years ago, you still had to work for a bit of publicity, because the cameras came out only if you were walking a red carpet or making some kind of promotional appearance. We weren't stalked the way celebrities are stalked nowadays. It seemed to me to just be a much more civilized, respectful time, in terms of the relationship between stars and the press.

I feel pretty lucky that my separation from Peter largely went under the radar for as long as it did, that I was able to live up at the ranch with the girls in relative solitude, far away from all the clamoring for the "money" shot. In more ways than one, the girls and I really did live off the grid for those two years; those crucial months allowed us to get grounded, get our balance back, reinforce ourselves while our family changed—me and my little pack of fierce women. It was a great place to fall apart and begin to put the pieces back together. I will forever be grateful for that time, despite how very difficult and frightening it was—especially at the end, when the full realization that my marriage was over finally hit me.

When Peter filed for divorce in the spring of 2012, things just became way, way more complicated, in terms of navigating this huge life transition, especially when the media caught hold of the news.

Never mind the packs of paparazzi that started following me, wanting to know how I felt. Of course, at times I felt like shouting out my own questions, like, "How do you think I feel, having my marriage end, my family be forever changed?" It seemed like all the tabloid shooters wanted to do was capture my sadness on camera, so they could then sell it to the highest bidder. The goal seemed to be to get the shot of me looking weepy or distraught or just heavy and tired. Then it would be paired up with some made-up sad-sack story that didn't at all represent what any of us were actually going through.

I look at the photos taken of me during that time now, and I just feel so sorry for that version of me. I look like a deer caught in the headlights, just before the crash actually happens.

Fortunately, the celebrity "news" cycle is fast. My news became old news and gradually the paparazzi lost interest in me. For the most part.

I mean, here I am, a full year and a half later—we've all moved on, we've all begun to settle into our new lives, yet . . . there are still a handful of photographers, which is, mercifully, a small number, who think that getting a photograph of me is somehow going to help pay for their kids' college.

These are the guys who ambush me while I'm walking my youngest to school, or who follow me, after school drop-off, to the nearest gas station, and they snap away while I'm wearing sweats and pumping gas. I call these guys the "shooters," as they've kind of broken off from the pack and are lone wolves, out there looking to get their money shot at eight a.m. I can't stand it that these guys think it's all right to track me and my kids like this, though, for the record, my girls just think they're dumb and ignore them. I have to work hard not to lash out—especially when they might actually hurt someone, like the genius who follows me by riding in the backseat of a car with blacked-out windows, and who thinks nothing of having his driver bang a U-turn in the middle of a three-lane street so he can shoot me while I walk into the grocery store. But here's the thing: They're just waiting—waiting—for me to lash out, so they can get the picture of me going off the deep end. That's the shot that they're all after: catching me losing my composure. So my job—in these moments—is to not react. To give them nothing. This may mean stifling a yawn or resisting the urge to scratch. Or it might mean buying just a half a tank of gas, instead of a full one, so I can get the hell out of there.

By now, of course, I can sense when a "shooter" is anywhere in the vicinity. It's as though I can smell them—even when they're pretty far away. I've been known to be walking along with Mr. Showbiz and will whisper under my breath, "Shooter at eight o'clock!" And of course he's completely oblivious and he'll start craning his neck and saying, "Where? Where?" Every single time, he seems genuinely surprised when a picture of us shows up on some crappy Web site the next day. He's still, after all these years, one of the lucky ones who has never gotten used to this.

I, on the other hand, haven't been so lucky. Lately, I've lost my Zen cool where the shooters are concerned, and so I've taken to wearing hoodies in order to provide myself with some level of protection, since these guys hide out inside parked cars, for God's sake. So I have lots of hoodies in many different colors, because I like variety. When I wake up and I sense that the shooters are out there, before I head out the door, I just hood up, and miraculously I become way less desirable to the camera. It's almost as if I'm invisible. Who knew? It's the best anti-paparazzi wear going. Whoever said diamonds are a girl's best friend was talking about another time, another era; I'm here to tell you that in this crazy town, hoodies are a girl's best friend.

HOME ALONE

The first time my girls went to stay at their father's house, I had no idea what to do with myself.

There is a lot of romanticizing that goes on around this particularly rugged rite of passage: the first time your kids go to your divorced spouse's place to spend the night. To some—particularly, say, your still-married friends who have a houseful of small children—there's this crazy, hyper-romanticized idea that once you drop the kids off, or wave good-bye and close the front door, you're going to pop the cork on an iced-up bottle of bubbly, blast music from the long-neglected sound track of your own youth at an insanely high volume, and then dance around your place with the abandon of a crazed, dizzy-with-freedom pixie.

Well, I am here to tell you that this is not what happens. At all. Instead, you close that door and immediately you feel about ten tons heavier. You do not feel free, and no burden of any size whatsoever has miraculously been lifted. No sense of relief at not being Mom for the first time in fifteen years descends; no curiosity about reconnecting with your long-neglected self takes hold. There's just this awful, dull ache where your now-kid-free heart used to be, and the emptiness of your arms feels like a particularly nasty kind of amputation. In short, it does not feel good. It hurts. Terribly. And for me, at least, it was right up there with the worst things I've ever experienced.

How on earth can anyone prepare for this moment? How can you ready yourself for sending your babies off to be with their dad when that means that they're not going to be with . . . you, too?

In an instant, I got that this was the kind of I-don't-wish-this-on-anyone-else moment that can easily lead a woman to drink, overeat, or numb her pain with some kind of sinister substance. It was the kind of moment in which the dark side beckons and any woman would be hard-pressed to resist.

And I was no different.

But before these or any other destructive options could flash through my mind, I looked down and noticed something: There was a smudge of dirt on one of the white tiles on the floor of my all-white kitchen. I bent down to take a closer look, and lo and behold, there was another speck of dirt on another tile, and another and . . . the floor was filthy!

So I did what any woman who finds herself home alone for the first time in more than a decade (actually, almost two) would do: I got out a toothbrush and a bottle of bleach, and I got to work. I spent the next however long (I lost all track of time) on my hands and knees, scrubbing each tile with an intensity that would put Mr. Clean to shame. But that was just the start: When I felt like no tile had gone untouched, I then went to work on the tiny tracks of grout that anchored those tiles. I went at those yards and yards of caulking as if my life depended on it. I worked in a methodical clockwork spiral, beginning in the middle of the floor, and I did not look up until I had bumped, quite literally, into the oven anchored against one wall. By then I was utterly spent and the floor was gleaming like an ice-skating rink just after the Zamboni has passed through. I looked up at the clock and realized that almost three hours had passed. I was drenched in sweat and my hands hurt. It was time for a bathroom break and a drink of water.

Now that I look back on this, I realize that I might've come across as a woman who had a pretty serious case of OCD, and you know what? That night I guess I did. I experienced the absence of my girls like a loud bell ringing, and ringing, and ringing, and the only way I could turn it off was to scrub that floor until it looked like it had just been installed that afternoon.

I scrubbed that floor like a mad cleaning lady because I had absolutely no clue on earth how to just be on my own.

There. I said it. I had no idea at all how to just be alone with myself.

No one ever tells you that you have to have a bit of a plan of action for this particularly cruel moment when the universe reaches down and tears your mom suit right off of your back, leaving you standing there naked and utterly lost and confused.

After my bathroom break and a drink of water, I remember I did feel a bit better. And absolutely bone-tired. This was good. Because the only thing I felt any confidence at all in being able to do was sleep. So I put the cap back on the bleach, tossed the toothbrush, and turned off the lights. As I snuggled in, I willed myself to think happy thoughts, such as, *Just think how nice it's going to be to wake up to such a clean kitchen floor!* so that the vast aloneness surrounding me wouldn't swallow me up.

Thank God I did sleep that night, but it was strange, like sleeping in a vacant house. Every cell of my own body missed the cells of those three precious bodies. It took me a while to settle down, but when I did, I slept the deepest, blackest sleep of my life.

I woke up to my phone ringing. It was my girls, calling me to say good morning.

I could do this. I could.

GETTING TO KNOW
THE GIRL IN THE MIRROR

What do you do when you hit rock bottom? Run—run, I say—to the bathroom and look at yourself in the mirror. I am not kidding.

But first, I think the better question is, What do you do when you don't hit rock bottom? What do you do when you keep bashing your head against the craggy rocks of life over and over and over again? What if you don't hit bottom and so you never get to learn to recognize that you just keep hurting yourself?

It's all about getting wise to the pattern. The repetition. The constant doing of things that don't serve you. Recognizing, finally, the voice in your head that doesn't serve you, that keeps you trapped.

Only hitting bottom can break all this shit up.

It starts, I think, somewhere around early adolescence, or at least that's where it started for me. I think of it as the "point of impact," that moment in time when something so profoundly unsettling happens that something vital and deep inside gets flipped upside down and spun out of balance. It could be any number of things: a change in your family structure by death or divorce, the loss of your home, or financial troubles—or any combination of these. Or it could be something more horrific, like abuse, neglect, or molestation. Whatever it is, it disrupts the flow and creates kind of a dam that keeps the waters from moving freely in and out of the beautiful, flowing river of your soul.

For me, knowing that the point of impact is usually during childhood makes me feel incredibly sad. It's amazing how oblivious we tend to be to the suffering of those around us, especially the smallest and youngest among us. Don't get me wrong: We don't miss the signs of sadness or sorrow or loss or confusion on purpose. I think our brains are kind of designed to persevere, even when we may need a helping hand. At least, mine was.

The point of impact for me was my dad's first heart attack, when I was nine years old. From that moment on, my family changed. Every decision that was made going forward was made with my dad's failing health in mind. His heart attack led to my family being torn apart. My dad's poor health caused us financial hardship and forced both my mom and dad to scramble to find new careers. In response to this, I think that on some level, I decided that I should start taking care of myself and, if possible, contribute what I could, even financially, to the greater good of the family.

This meant that I became incredibly stoic, which is an acceptable way of saying . . . I learned how to shut down emotionally pretty early on. It wasn't until I met Peter that I was able to let my guard down again, and even being married to him and having children and all the emotional support and opportunity that provided me couldn't get to what had been locked up for so long. No amount of love from the outside was going to break that dam that held back my heart. Only I could do that. If only I knew how.

I had become a master at coping. As my mother once said, I could do appropriate very well, meaning I just didn't let anyone, myself included, see what was really going on inside. I mastered the cool, slightly disapproving mask, which always seemed to signal to the world that I was in control and unruffled, when in fact I was dying inside.

This was true when I was young and had to leave Illinois for Arizona. It was true when I found myself in LA working eighteen hours a day when I very well could, and possibly should, have been in high school. And it was most heartbreakingly true when my husband was working across the country for long stretches of time and I was home in LA caring for our kids and missing him so much, but not knowing how to reach out to him and tell him that I wasn't doing so well being both mom and dad on my own with three young kids.

I just didn't have any freaking clue how to raise the white flag. Instead I'd isolate myself and push the people I loved and needed the most away—especially him.

The two years or so leading up to the divorce were the worst, in terms of my being stuck in this emotionally withdrawn coping mode. Peter was really coming into his own as an actor, but his work was either always on the East Coast or up in Canada, and so we didn't get to see him very much, and definitely not as much as I needed. But despite how busy he was, he'd always fly home whenever he could, even when it meant landing and spending *less than a day* with me and the girls.

During these short visits, instead of rushing toward him like I really wanted to, I'd pull back and kind of fade into the background, telling myself the girls needed his time and attention more than I did. Then he'd leave, and I'd be flooded with feelings of anger and resentment and blame. I'd get so mad that I'd pull away even further, and so I'd unconsciously create this vicious cycle of withholding myself from him, withholding my feelings and my fears and my needs in a way that is certain to cause harm to any relationship. Being stoic, I've learned the hard way, is the death of intimacy.

That period of our marriage totally sucked for me, just as I know it did for him. I was sad and lonely and overwhelmed, and I missed and needed my husband, but I was so deeply embedded in the dysfunctional coping I'd learned so early on that I couldn't see the forest for the trees. And it cost me. It cost me everything. And so I lost the thing I valued the most. I lost my marriage.

Only then did I hit bottom. And I hit it hard, thank you very much.

At first, when I did hit that bottom, it sucked more than anything I've ever experienced before, and it was only when I began to pull myself together, broken bit by broken bit, that I realized this was actually the best thing that had ever happened to me. You need to get shattered in order to put yourself back together properly. The trick, though, is not to try to glue the pieces back into the same old places and in the same old pattern. The better way is to learn and grow and be brave enough to take on a new shape, a new outlook, a new wisdom. God, I wish I'd known this sooner. I really, really do. But you learn only when you are ready to learn.

In Buddhism, they call this repetitive pattern of tripping up *samsara*, which is the continual cycle of life and death and rebirth that we all go through countless times during the course of our own lives. The goal—in Buddhism, as it is with anyone who wants to grow up and be free to love and live fully—is to break this awful cycle, to get out of the way of *samsara* and be free to live in the moment, authentically and passionately.

This can happen only by hitting bottom. At least, that's been my own experience. It wasn't until I found myself sobbing on that kitchen floor in a puddle of bleach, with a toothbrush in my hand, that I was honestly able to give in to the overwhelming realization that I had just been *coping* my whole life, not really living, not even really *feeling*.

I had first learned to cope when my dad got sick. Then I had to learn to cope when I was getting my ass handed to me on the playground of a strange middle school in a strange state. Then I had to cope with dipping my toe into acting and then finding myself pulled into the whirling tornado of teenage fame. Then I learned to cope with having a baby early in a relationship that was too new for me to know whether we were meant to make it or not, but yet we did make it. We kept on together and built a beautiful life together, a beautiful family. Then I lost my dad and coped again, sort of, but then things began to unravel. I tried my best to cope some more. By then my style of coping wasn't working at all, but it was all I knew. . . . Oh, my God . . . when I reread this paragraph, I realize . . . that was an awful lot of coping! And it was a lot of coping until it was just too damn much, and I couldn't cope anymore.

I had to stop coping and start to get real, and the only way I could do that was to go within and finally contend with that original point of impact. I had to go back, resurrect my young self, and finally acknowledge how hurt, lost, and unloved she'd felt, and how I'd carried these unresolved feelings around with me, and how they'd kept me from being free.

I know how incredibly corny and clichéd this is all starting to sound, and I have to admit that even I hear Stuart Smalley, the fantastic character created by Al Franken on *SNL*, whispering in my ear, "I'm good enough. I'm smart enough. And, doggone it, people like me." But really, he was onto something there. Trust me: Standing in front of the mirror and addressing your younger self works. It really, truly does. When I realize that I'm slipping into "coping" mode, I take the time to look in the mirror and see past my adult self and reconnect with the very young me, the girl with the long white braids and the buckteeth. When I'm lucky, and patient, I see her in there, and when I do catch a glimpse of that part of me, I tell her that I know she felt alone and overwhelmed, but that she's really not—that I'm here for her, and that I love her, and I won't leave her, and together we will figure this out.

I'm new at this, for sure. And I definitely tend to take one step forward, two steps back. But I know I've got the skills to learn this kind of self-love. I mean, all I have to do is look at my own children, who still need and want nurturing and love and reassurance from me. It's so easy and natural for me to give it to them. . . . I guess it's time to turn some of that maternal love in on myself.

I used to be the girl who rolled her eyes whenever someone would think he or she was being helpful by sharing the horseshit line, "You'll never truly be able to love someone else until you truly love yourself." I would, whether it was coming from a therapist, a shaman, a fortune cookie, or my own mother, shut that message out and then shut right down. But you know what? That old pearl just so happens to be true. And if you don't believe, do what I did and take a good long look in the mirror. It might just change your life.

STALKING THE ELUSIVE
HAPPY FAMILY

S o there I was, slogging my way through the five stages of grief, which are generally understood to be denial, anger, bargaining, depression, and acceptance. Of course, there's a lot of other stuff that you have to dig through and digest besides the "big five," but I'd say this is a pretty helpful checklist, especially in those early days when you're walking around pretty dazed and confused.

Initially it felt like I had somehow been ejected from a very exclusive club, and at first I didn't have a clue why. All I knew was that I'd find myself, say, in the grocery store, standing behind an older couple. I'd immediately notice that they both had on wedding bands, and I'd watch as they'd help each other unload their basket and arrange their items on the conveyor belt. If I was lucky, I might catch a glimpse of the husband gently putting his hand on his wife's back, or I'd see her smile gratefully at his gallantry. I'd sigh as they gathered up their purchases and made their way to the door. I'd be watching them so intently that

I'd find myself holding up the line, where I'd be yearning to drop my potato bread and chase after them and ask, "How is it that you love each other so beautifully? What is the magic ingredient that keeps you so tenderly bound together?" Before I could do this, though, I'd be ripped from my daydream by an important question: "Paper or plastic?"

I just couldn't get enough of these sightings.

I became something of a happy-couple stalker. If it makes me seem a little less pathetic, I can pretend I was doing it for somewhat scientific reasons, like a bird-watcher, or maybe character research for a new role, but whatever compelled me, I'd find myself drawn to a happy couple or family. I'd gravitate toward them, maneuvering myself into their orbit as though somehow, if I got close enough, I'd be pulled into their magic force field of love and familial unity and I would somehow be healed by this. I'd move into their space and gratefully breathe in that unique pheromone happy families give off. If nothing else, I always felt warmed up and fortified by this kind of encounter, benefiting from the unspoken joy and contentment that drew me to these people.

More than once, a member of a family would eye me suspiciously, wondering, I'm sure, *Who the hell is this grown woman who is getting just a little too close?* At this point, I would just blurt out how happy they all seemed, how lucky they were to have one another, and I'd back away, waving, thanking them, always with aching sincerity. Those lucky people! I so badly wanted what they had that more than once one of my daughters would have to pull me away, laughing at the fact that I'd have this weird, dreamy look on my face and sometimes even tears in my eyes.

And this is why I think there's actually a sixth, unacknowledged stage of grief that we have to go through, at least when it comes to the grieving that happens when your family is broken up after so many years together: pure longing. The *missing* of it all. The yearning for what was—or what you once thought (and hoped) had been there. I was floored by how much I missed the idea and the actual fact of an "us." I missed being part of an intact, traditional family. And, for a while there, I was drowning in how badly I still yearned for it.

Getting through these phases was going to take some time, I realized. And it might, it began to dawn on me, also take some time to begin to wrap my head around the idea, the fact, that I was now single. Single? Are you f*@king kidding me!? I did not like the sound of that at all! Eventually, figuring out how to step into all of this change would come to me.

But for right then I just needed to be willing to sit there, in the middle of it all, and feel it. And I'd keep my eye out for those who had what I wanted, and I'd keep hoping that their happy-familyness would rub off on me.

WHO'S THAT GIRL?

There are moments in life when you get to take a good, hard look at yourself. I had one of those when my marriage was coming to an end. Actually, I had several, so many that I cannot even begin to count them. But despite how many of them I had, it wasn't until Peter finally pulled the trigger and filed for divorce that I actually got it.

Here's what would happen before then: I'd catch a glimpse of myself in the mirror and I'd think, *Ewwww. I don't look so great. Am I really that tired? Am I really carrying all that junk in the trunk?* and so I'd cringe and feel lousy, and then I'd hustle away from that mirror as fast as I possibly could and I'd kind of force myself to forget what I'd just caught a glimpse of.

I had been in a certain kind of self-imposed hiatus for several years at that point. I'd made the decision to step away from my career and put all of my focus on raising our three girls. I'd wanted us all to move up to our ranch while my dad was still alive, but we missed out on that, and then I'd wanted that with Peter, and . . . well, you know how that turned out.

I just really, really wanted all of us to be together, to fulfill this ardent, deep wish I had to have all the people I loved best in the world close to one another, caring for one another.

All of my reasons for going to the country were, on the face of it, quite noble and good, but my altruism, my idealism, like it does for so many of us women, slowly got the best of me when I stubbornly held on to it, ignoring—much to my own detriment—what was actually going on around me.

I truly thought that bringing my girls up to the country and putting them in a small, rural public school and giving them open space and big starry nights and no stress would be good for them—and me. And it was. To a point. But without my knowing it, I began to hide out up there; I kept way too much of what was really happening for me hidden. I was pouring all of my energies into the girls—totally at the expense of taking care of myself.

Peter was working his head off then, mostly on the East Coast, and I thought that, since he was basically only flying in for weekends, he could fly in closer to the ranch and just visit us there. Reasonable, right? But this was much harder in practice—for both him and us—than I thought it would be.

My planting us up in the country meant he would have to add at least two hours of extra travel to get up to the ranch from the city, so he'd get to us after flying across the country tired but always so, so happy to see the girls. He'd arrive with all of this awesome daddy energy, and the girls would go nuts. Then, just like that, he'd have to leave again (usually after just one or two days) and it would take, I now can see, a crazy amount of emotional work on my part—more than I could've imagined—to smooth out the edges around those visits, helping the girls transition back into our daily life, which would go on without him. It was hard. It was hard on us all. And it was hard on me in ways that I just didn't understand back then.

I felt like I was spending all of my energy holding down the fort, and I was, but pretty soon the fort started to get hold of me, too. My stoicism started to work against me, and before too long, it became clear that something was going to have to give.

When you become so single-minded, when you really put the blinders on—which, in my case, was to focus on being the most attentive, available mother that I possibly could be—other vital needs go unattended to, and this, we all know (though we usually find out only with the benefit of hindsight, and we usually get that hindsight only after we've been hit with some giant, gnarly, cosmic wake-up call, like your spouse filing for divorce) is never, ever a good thing.

It's the yin and yang of it all, keeping the old teeter-totter balanced, if you will. Sure, I had solitude up there on the ranch, but when the kids weren't with me, that solitude, if I'm honest about it, became isolation. I was hiding out. I wasn't in the game. I wasn't really living my life. And it was beginning to show. I stopped taking care of myself and just wore sweats or barn clothes. I felt sluggish and . . . old. In other words, I was depressed. And worn down. And my body was just packing on the pounds as a reaction to all that.

And that was why I'd avoid mirrors. And shopping. And going anywhere that would entail my having to dress up—because all of my nicest clothes were now too tight. I just looked the other way, looked past myself, for as long as I possibly could.

But then, after a good couple of years of this, I just couldn't look away anymore.

I know that I'm not alone in this. So many of us moms, without even knowing it, just kind of let ourselves go. I don't just mean that we stop putting on makeup, or mindlessly eat what's left on our kids' plates, or start to wear the same yoga pants four days running, and rubber bands become our favorite hair accessories. There is all that, of course. But what I mean is that we let our innermost self—our warrior woman, hot-mama, sexy-goddess self—check out on us. When this happens, we get heavy: heavy of heart, heavy of thought, heavy of butt.

Believe me, I know.

I was heavy all the way around. I found that, after two years up at the ranch, I had become pretty low-functioning. There was no doubt that I was depressed, and what little energy I had, the girls got. But you know what? They deserved more than that. And one day it hit me that I, too, deserved more than that.

I couldn't just stay in bed, pull up the covers, and wait for life to come wake me up. I was going to have to do that by—and for—myself.

I think, in some distant lands, they call this learning to take good care of yourself, growing up.

Life had thrown me a curveball. So what was I going to do about it? I could either duck or I could take a swing at it.

It struck me as pretty funny that once I got myself upright and decided to take charge of my physical health and eat clean and commit to regular exercise—which, by the way, I hated—I started to lose weight. Pretty soon the headlines were blaring things like, "Jennie Garth on Heartbreak Diet!" or "Garth Rail-thin Due to Divorce Diet!"

It all became pretty dramatic and, as usual, a way for the tabloids to make some hay with what they thought was my life, but really?

What I was actually getting rid of was my "sad fat."

I had been unhappy—just as Peter had been—for several years, and I finally realized that I could either stay buried by that unhappiness, which was not just wrapped around my heart but clinging to my hips and thighs, or I could buck up and get moving and get on with my life. I could figure out how to heal myself, body and soul. No one said it was going to be easy, and it never is. Ever.

I started, tiny baby step by tiny baby step, to take care of myself. I started to cry, and to talk, and to eat healthier, and to exercise, and to live again. And as I did, the weight of it all began to lift.

I'm now thirty pounds lighter. And that's a relief, because now I've got some energy to begin to tackle the really heavy-duty stuff. Like getting back out there and making a meaningful go of it, making a meaningful new life for myself. It will be a challenge, but I am not one to shy away from a good challenge. Ever.

THROW THIS HOUSE
OUT THE WINDOW

To make our return to the maddening craziness that is LA, we had to begin all over again. Our family home back in LA, the one we'd bought together and had nested in with our kids, was being rented out. So now I had to find a new place for me and the girls to live.

Coming back to LA was bracing. Not just because I was coming back single, but because we had been gone for two full years, which in Hollywood time is about a hundred years. I had been planted in the middle of *quiet* for so long. I had forgotten about the traffic and the noise and all the hullabaloo of the business. These things, I realized, would take some getting used to again.

So the question became where to plant us while I experienced reentry and got reacclimated to my LA life.

Finally, some good luck! Right away I found a great small house that exuded a peaceful, positive vibe. It was close enough to Peter's place, pretty close to school, and it was secluded enough to give us some much-needed privacy, so I signed the lease. It's a midcentury house, so it's unfussy and open, but it's got only one bathroom, and for the girls, well, that in and of itself is quite a challenge. And it's got some other older-house issues as well.

For instance, it's got the worst water pressure of any house I've ever lived in. It's definitely one of those places where you cannot flush the toilet while someone is in the shower, which, for us, means pretty much all the time. And if you want to make a cup of tea, you need to make sure you have a spare fifteen minutes just to fill the kettle up with water before you can even put it on to boil.

And it's cold. Yes—believe it or not, it gets downright chilly here in LA, especially at night, after the sun goes down. So often, in the morning, we'll all stagger around, wrapped up in big blankets, thick socks on, while we pull ourselves together before heading off to school and work.

Oh. And the electric gate's been on the fritz, too. And the Internet works sporadically, usually at really odd times of the day or night, and so it's not unusual to see one or another of us, head down, laptop in hand, trying to find a hot—or even lukewarm—spot so we can get enough of a signal to check e-mail or surf the Web.

For girls, we're a pretty low-maintenance bunch, though, and so we make this house work. For example, if the TV goes on the fritz, since none of us has any idea what to do, we'll just go without TV until I remember that I need to call the cable guy and get him to come over and push that restart button on the back of the cable box for us.

Still, while we've managed to acclimate and get back in the swing of things, we've had our share of heartbreak at this sweet reentry house, too: Our beloved cat, Gizmo, an indoor guy, somehow or another got out, and after we walked around for a while wondering, "Where's Gizmo?" we got our answer soon enough when we realized he'd gotten out and, disoriented by this new and unfamiliar place he'd found himself in, was tragically hit by a car. Poor Gizmo had really dug life on the ranch, because there were no cars and there were lots of mice, and he could go in and out without a thought. Losing him was a terrible blow to us all, and I know that forever, for all of us, Gizmo and this little house will be bound together in our minds and hearts.

But you know what? Despite that tragedy, and though from time to time I find myself telling the girls I'd like to take this house and throw it out the window, I really do kind of love this place. By and large it's been good to us, and it's been a sweet, safe, transitional landing pad for me and the girls as we adjust and reconfigure ourselves as a family.

Just recently we sold our old LA family home. I think I expected to feel really sad at that moment, to feel as though I were closing a favorite chapter, or even getting to the very end of a beloved book, and I did get a little weepy when I took a final lonely walk-through, but what I mostly felt was gratitude and thanks for all that house had given me, had given us. It was something we had created, and I felt incredibly proud of all that house had represented and been. It had been a very good house. A very good home.

Just a few days after letting go of the old house, I closed on a new house. My new house. Our new house! It's a total project, but this is what makes it so important to me: I am going to renovate that house top to bottom, just like I did our last house. In my mind's eye, I can see how to refine it so that it better supports us and better reflects the life I aspire to as a mom and as an independent woman: a life that is open, relaxed, playful, and yet solid.

It feels good to be reactivating this part of myself, the part that feels confident taking down a few walls and working with contractors, builders, and craftsmen. It's feels like I'm going back to some vital part within myself. It's about reviving an important muscle, the muscle I need to look ahead and to help me build a future.

It's going to be a good thing, this new house of ours, and I can even, from time to time, catch a glimpse of us there, down the road, when the girls are coming back from college, or from their far-flung, interesting, and independent lives. They will know that this new place, this place we have yet to live in, will always be their home.

But like everything these days, the renovation will take time. Everything, it seems, is a process.

Until then, I won't throw this little house away—at least, not just yet. We'll stay here in our rented hideaway, with the dribbly water and chilly morning floors, and we'll love being here, being together, we four, safe, sound, and snug.

DOG ABOUT TOWN

A couple of years ago, for Christmas, we got the girls a dog: a big, floppy Labradoodle puppy. We named her "the Black Pearl" because of her lustrous, shiny black curls, and just because it's such an awesome name. We call her Pearl for short.

Pearl's pretty much full-grown now and she's about the size of a miniature horse. She's still superyoung at heart and is, in many ways, still all puppy, even though she's so giant. I think it's fair to say that she's pretty high-maintenance and has some settling in to do, which means that she's definitely not quite ready to be left alone. In fact, in many ways Pearl's kind of my fourth daughter—the challenging, exasperating, slobbery one. Not infrequently, after a long day with her, I feel like I could use a therapy session (or two).

Pearl's my constant companion, not just because I like her company (which I sort of do), but because she would lose her mind if she were left home alone. So, whenever I go out to do errands, Pearl comes along.

I take Pearl with me everywhere so I can keep a close eye on her, so that I know she's staying, to the degree that she can, on the relative straight and narrow. When she's a little older—and so a bit more independent and more laid-back (please, God)—I'll think about leaving her home alone.

But until then, it's me and Pearl.

She likes riding in the car, but for some reason she won't get into the car on her own, so I have to coax her to at least try; then, when she's ready, I hunker down behind her and push/hoist her up and into the vehicle. And she's massive! I always say, "Get your big butt up there, Pearl!" But she just looks at me with her dopey eyes and kind of sits back into my hands and makes the whole affair kind of pathetic.

And then off we go: I take her hiking with me, while shuttling the girls around, to the grocery store—she's even been known to show up in some of the finer restaurants in town. Yes. You heard that right.

But let's be clear about something: I never, ever play the celebrity card where Pearl is concerned. In fact, I pretty much never play that card at all. That's just not my style. The truth is, I'm not a very good rule breaker; I always seem to get caught red-handed. And I'm lousy at doing the diva thing. And this isn't about diva antics anyway; this is about doing what I have to do to keep Pearl alive and breathing.

This means that our Black Pearl is a registered "service" dog, having received her certificate and her official vest. She's an "emotional" support dog, which means I get to take her with me everywhere, so I can provide her with emotional support.

Pearl—who does, by the way, occasionally wear a string of pearls, which look superglamorous against her black fur—isn't very good at sitting still. Or if she does sit still, she's still got to be busy. For example, one time, when I met a friend for drinks at a pretty popular restaurant, before I knew it she'd managed to almost chew the leg off one of the wooden chairs at the table next to us. I had no choice but to make mine a double, and I don't think I've been back to that particular restaurant since—at least not with Pearl.

Pearl is giant, but she takes up the space of three dogs her size, particularly when she decides she's going to sleep on my bed. I don't know quite how to describe what it's like to sleep with her, except to say that it's hot and dog-breathy and yet utterly endearing and difficult to say no to. In this way, she's definitely my baby: the one who gets away with murder.

Can't live with her, can't live without her—that's my Pearl.

LICKING THE BOTTOM OF MY SHOE

I thought I could avoid it. I really did. But I can't possibly write this book without writing about . . . dating. Right? But I want the record to show that I acknowledge that dating, for most of us, ranks right up there with having to go for the annual Pap smear or having to try on a bathing suit in February. It's uncomfortable, awkward, and it can send us back to the couch and Netflix and potato chips faster than just about anything else.

I was married for *so* long that, once I recovered from the initial shock of finding myself single again, whenever anybody suggested that I might want to get out there and start dating, well, I would quite literally start hyperventilating.

I mean, what is this thing called dating? What does it mean to meet a strange man and have a drink or dinner or do whatever it is that people do when they go on dates? The whole idea of having to do what I had never actually done—*ever in my whole life*—just completely freaked me out.

The truth is, I had been the poster girl for old married lady for so long that my brain would just freeze when I even attempted to say the word *date*. I mean, come on: I married for the first time when I was twenty-two, and then for the second time when I was twenty-eight, which might not sound that young, but . . . wait! I was already a mother at twenty-five when I made my way down the aisle for the second time. So in married-lady years, I was old—like, ancient-dog-years married-lady old. I had been off the market so long that I had never actually been on the market. And I mean this sincerely. I had not had a date since I was a kid, and that doesn't count, because I was a kid. I had no muscle memory for the dating thing, no reference point for it. But everyone around me persisted. "You've got to get back out there! You've got to get back on the horse!" I guess that's one way of putting it. But here's the thing: From my perspective, I had a pretty huge handicap when it came to entering the dating pool. I would never be able to go on a "date" on anything even remotely close to a level playing field, thanks to our friend the Internet.

Just think about it: A friend wants to set me up with a friend of a friend's brother-in-law, and so I reasonably ask, "Okay, what's he like?" I get a one-word response, like, "Nice," or, "Hot."

Whereas the guy in question, he gets to Google me. He gets to find out every last detail of my life, including all of those really crazy, juicy intimate things that aren't even true. And images to accompany those facts! Images from when I was sixteen till now!

Despite this, let's say I agree to meet Mr. Hot. We sit down to dinner, and before I can politely ask, "So, what do you do for a living?" Mr. Hot blurts out: "Is it true you coldcocked Shannen Doherty at the Emmys?" Of course not, but hello! Where on earth is the conversation supposed to go from there?

This is precisely why I've gone on the record as saying I'd rather lick the bottom of a dirty shoe than go on a date. The tabloids got one right!

But you know what? When I became single again, I was thirty-nine years old, and if I really wasn't going to go on a date ever again, that meant I might end up roaming this planet for another, oh, forty or fifty years without getting close enough to a man to even *smell* him, and this would not be a good thing at all, because the truth of the matter is, I love the way men smell. I really, honest-to-God do. I love so many things about them, because I just love them. I just don't understand them all that well.

To complicate things, I am one of those women who is unapologetically attracted to the bad boys. Wait a minute. . . . That's not entirely true; let me clarify. I am attracted to men who look like they *might* be bad boys, but who are really total sweethearts under the scruffy, I-will-not-take-any-shit-from-anyone exterior. I want to find someone who will be incredibly good to me, but who looks like he might not be that great to me. Follow?

Immediately postsplit, I was ill prepared to face the dating abyss on my own, since I was going through serious doubt about whether I knew anything at all about men. In the end, I realized that I knew *nothing at all*, so I would have to rely on my friends to help me work my way into the land of dating. I would need to turn to someone who had been through what I was going through now, to talk to someone who had also been in a longish marriage, with kids—but who had also wound up divorced. So I turned to my friend Luke. He would know what this terrifying time was all about. Or at least he would be someone of the opposite sex whose big, strong shoulder I could comfortably and safely rest my weary head on, while he explained the world of "man" to me.

But before we even had the chance to get together and properly catch each other up, there we were, all over the rags. "Kelly and Dylan, Together at Last!" Or "Luke Perry and Jennie Garth—Dating!"

I hate to burst the torrid Kelly-and-Dylan fantasy you're about to lose yourself in, but what we were really doing at some no-name coffee shop looked something like this: Luke would be trying to boost my confidence, usually encouraging me that it might be wise to get out of my sweatpants and brush my hair, while lecturing me on needing to go after the right kind of guy. See, he has always been very disapproving of my choices . . . always. Which I've found endearing, because he holds me in very high regard and thinks I deserve the best. So . . . maybe . . . I should start listening to him?

We would talk about relationships and what one ought to look for in a partner and yada-yada . . . and while the tabloids were thinking they were onto something igniting between us, Luke would be texting his lovely, long-term partner, and I would shrug off all of his suggestions about eligible guys who might be worth a look, while I twirled my bed-heady, less-than-clean hair.

In the midst of all the hoopla about the possibility that Luke and I might be a little more than just good friends, I actually did dip my toe into the murky, dark dating pool, and so I felt compelled, being the shy yet open book that I am, to address the Luke rumors head-on. So when someone asked me whether I was dating Luke, I snorted and said, "I can't date Luke. It would be too weird." Of course, this appeared on the newsstands the very next day.

What I was trying to say was that Luke had been one of my closest friends for more than half my life, and that I didn't want to even begin to jeopardize that friendship by ever giving anyone the impression that there was more than that between us. But it didn't really come out like that, especially when I immediately followed up that "weird" comment with, "But we do have incredible chemistry." I confused even myself with that one!

One of the things I had to face before I could get back out there and date was the fact that I had a very screwed-up sense of the love equation. I'm not talking about the kind of unconditional love I have for my children and which has already withstood the usual gamut of challenges—and which, as they all lurch through their teens, will be tested beyond belief. No, despite all of that, my love for them will last for all time.

I'm talking about the romantic kind, the kind I seem to have such a jinxed relationship with. I recently saw a shaman, and she suggested that instead of equating love with pain, which is what I used to do, I ought to work to equate love with power. Love equals power.

When someone with magical powers such as my shaman offers me insight like this, I try my best to take it, but it's as though I'm hearing the words, but I just can't understand them. She really might as well have been speaking a foreign language.

The whole concept of love and power confuses me. When I try to think about it, my brain freezes up in a way that really makes me question the future of my spotty memory.

But maybe that's the point: Maybe I'm not supposed to think so hard about it; maybe I'm just not supposed to solve that particular riddle. Maybe that's the whole point of it. Maybe the love equation just is, like infinity, or pi, or $E = mc^2$, and no matter what is on either side of that equal sign, I know one thing: Love is supposed to feel good, damn good. Knowing that fills me with a pretty powerful feeling.

And then it happened. The getting-out-there-and-dating thing. It happened without my even being aware that it was happening. I was flying to New York to promote *A Little Bit Country*, and I was sitting up in first class, next to this really hunky DIY TV star, and I thought, *Hey! I can fix him up with Corrine*, who was sitting a few rows back. I kept trying to chat up Corrine and he kept trying to chat me up, and when we finally landed and were at the baggage carousel, he gallantly fetched our bags for us, and then he gave me a soul hug that nearly buried me and asked if he could call me. I was so stunned, I just said yes. And there I was all of a sudden, back in the dating game.

So I dated DIY guy for a few weeks, which offered me a much-needed distraction from the very public end to my marriage, and then there were a few more dates with a few more guys, but nothing significant, until . . . I met someone on Instagram.

A LITTLE TWITTER

I was beginning to get used to my single-mom status, and about a year into the split, I had dated a handful of guys. Though I now felt less nervous about going out on that dreaded first date, I still didn't have much of a clue about what I ought to be looking for in a guy, what I needed in a romantic partner. I realized that thinking my way to a solution wasn't the answer, so I decided to give it a rest. What I needed was a vacation. A real trip away from the girls, just for a few days, a trip where I could just be Jennie, solo, without worrying about anyone else. I needed a weekend off, a few days to lose myself in a crowd. So I went to Austin—to Austin City Limits, the music festival—with my good friend Stephanie. It felt so good to immerse myself in some great music and not worry about what was, or wasn't, happening at home.

We were having a blast, and one day I posted a picture on Instagram, and a musician who was performing at the festival made a really sweet comment about it, so then I made a comment about his com-ment, and then we started communicating by Instagram and then Twitter. This was all so very "of the moment" of me, and it was fun and flirty, and I felt all groovy and with it and so #thisishowthekidsdo itthesedays. This musician was witty, warm, and about ten years younger than me, but we moved our conversation from Twitter and texting to the actual phone, and after lots of beautiful and intense conversations over several weeks, we finally decided we ought to meet, and so he came to LA.

It was strange and interesting, because we had been courting each other via social media, and then there we were, face-to-face, and so we started getting to know each other all over again, but this time in per-son, and it felt really warm and special.

I found myself crazy attracted to this guy, who was so very different from the "type" of guy I'm usually drawn to. He was warm and kind and communicative in a way that I found irresistible. Being around him woke me up on several levels. And like that, I found myself in posses-sion of a beating heart, after months and months of flatlining.

What was this? I was drawn to this quirky guy who was not only about a decade younger than me, but he'd never been married himself, had no kids, had never dated an actor, and, on top of all that, he lived in another state. Oh, and he was a touring musician, so he was never in one place for very long.

From the beginning, the odds were stacked against us, but I got priceless, beautiful things from that intensely loving six-month rela-tionship: I found out that I could not just love a man again, but I could fall in love and genuinely care about someone again and feel all that passion and desire—all the good stuff.

Plus, I found out that there's a type of guy out there that I was really intrigued by: a man who wanted to be "all in" and who wanted an honest-to-God messy and complicated intimacy. This was both alluring and terrifying because . . .

Could I, the queen of keeping my cards tucked in my vest, respond in kind and really let someone get close?

I wasn't at all sure. But I wanted to find out.

SINGLE WITH A CAPITAL "S"

My short but deep relationship with the sweet musician convinced me that I very much want to be "in the game," and I want to learn how to love someone, and I want to be brave enough to let someone come in close and love me back, but . . .

First I needed to learn how to be single. I needed to learn how to be truly okay on my own, without a man there to give me a sense of security or a sense of being okay in the world. I had relied on that for so long that I didn't really trust that I could be okay without it; I had been coupled up for so long that I had lost faith in my ability to be alone, and to be alone well.

Being single, I finally came to realize, is the only real way to get down to business and face your flaws and demons and all that dark and sticky stuff that we all must, at some point or another, turn and face head-on. At least that's been true for me. I needed to be unattached to be able to figure out what went wrong when I was attached: how my expectations or my unmet needs or my fears or whatever got in the way of my being able to relate in the healthiest and most satisfying way possible, for both parties involved.

So I decided that, once I got over the shock of how sweet and meaningful and yet how brief my relationship with the musician had been, I would keep my eye out for a man who is kind and accountable and open and adventurous and dependable, and maybe he would look a little naughty, but first . . . I had to put the focus squarely on myself and begin to dismantle all the silly, unhealthy, and unhelpful notions I had about relationships and men.

This wasn't easy at first. I mean, really being with yourself can be tedious as all hell. But once I got past the initial awful, itchy part, I found that I was relaxing into things. At last. I found that I was finally getting the breather I had needed for so very long. I had found the silver lining in being single. I had begun to find myself.

NEVER SAY NEVER

I've never been an open book, as you can tell by now. And in writing this book, I threw myself over the proverbial cliff and I just went for it. For months and months I dug in and wrote my head off. And though what I was writing about was often extremely humbling, more than a bit revealing, and always, mercifully, illuminating, I kept my head down and kept at it. And then one day it was done. I finished the first draft of my manuscript and sent it off to my publisher.

And then . . . I swear to God . . . it just happened. Within days of writing "the end," I met someone. I met a man. A wonderful man. A grown-up man. A man who lives in the same state. A man who is lovely and luscious and funny and smart. And kind. He runs his own business and is superbusy, so he's respectful and understanding about how extremely busy my own life is. Recently I started renovating a house and I agreed to have this undertaking filmed for HGTV, which means I get a reality show "do-over," and this time it feels right. It feels good.

And, of course, I've got my three girls to look after and I've got other projects in the works and . . . and . . . and . . .

The upshot is, I have no idea where this new romantic thing is going, and there's a chance that by the time this book is actually bound and printed and in your hands things may be different in my personal life, but I'm absolutely certain of one thing: My status won't have changed. I will still be fully in my life, fully present, and fully engaged. On all fronts. And it will all be good.

And I won't, I am beginning to see, ever be alone again.

MISTAKEN IDENTITY

You know what's really awkward? When someone comes up to me and says, "Wow! You look just like Jennie Garth!" Or worse, "Wow! You look just like that girl Jenny, the one who wrote those parenting books and who used to pose for *Playboy* but is now on *The View*!" Or even worse still, "Hey! Are you that chick on that 913-something show? Well, you look exactly like her. I always hated that show and I hear she's a total bitch."

As you very well know by now, I am kind of a shy person. So when someone calls me out and tells me I look like Jennie Garth, meaning I look like myself, it's pretty easy for me to just smile and say, "Thank you," with some genuine gratitude. This is much easier than getting into the fact that I am actually her, because then the whole experience just blows wide-open and becomes too unpredictable, which can get really awkward for everyone involved, so I just do us all a favor and don't go there.

But if someone figures it out on their own, then there's usually a photo session with a smart phone, or maybe a request to call their friend in Nebraska, just to say hi, and they'll put me on the phone and then I'll have to try to convince the stranger I'm talking to that I'm really me and . . . you see? It's just way too confusing.

Those very occasional times when I actually do cop to being me, you'd be surprised by how many people want to argue with me about it. These exchanges usually go something like this:

"No way. You cannot be Jennie Garth."

"I am."

"No, you're not!"

"No, I am!"

"Shut up!"

"Okay."

At this point, oddly, this strange person telling me I'm not me usually becomes annoyed with me. That's why my go-to strategy of just saying thank you seems to work best for everybody.

When someone tells me I look like Jenny McCarthy, well, I've just never really known how to respond to that. I mean, the only things similar about us are our hair color and our names. (Even though they are spelled differently, and any Jennie or Jenny or Jenni will tell you in no uncertain terms that how she spells her name is highly important to her position in this world.) Jenny McCarthy is actually a friend of mine, and we've had several laughs over the years, because she has had the same thing happen to her, where people think she's me. She even got some mail of mine once, which is kind of scary, because that means that even the U.S. Postal Service confuses us from time to time.

But anyway, whenever someone confuses me with Jenny McCarthy, I'm kind of flattered, so I just smile and say, "Thank you!" and charge off without feeling like I've let them down in any way.

When someone tells me I look like that mean bitch on that show they hated, I usually do a quick visual sweep of wherever I am, just to see if there's any possibility I might make a run for it. This is when I tend to blank out for a second, the phrase "Help me!" running along the crawl in my mind, but when I come back to the moment, I just flash my gamest smile and offer a little chuckle to deflect the whole thing. Then I say, "Thank you."

That's my response even when I've been insulted multiple times by a complete stranger.

Thank you. It's such an important phrase when you're someone who is recognized on the street by people you don't know. I mean, what else can you say when someone approaches you when you're leaving Rite Aid with the deodorant and tampons you so desperately need? Let's look at several linguistic possibilities and options.

First, there's, "Fuck you!" but that's clearly not a very civilized, ladylike, or mindful way to behave in the world, and it's certainly not going to win me any fans, so that's not an option for me. Then there's, "Excuse me?" said with just the right amount of self-righteous indignation. But ninety-nine percent of the time, if you dare say this, people just assume you're a little deaf, and so they miss completely that you might be trying to shake them off, and they just repeat what they said, only louder, which only makes the whole encounter more awkward, and then other people usually start to stare, and . . . So why not be smart and just skip right to the "Thank you"?

Thank you in this context is kind of like the period at the end of the sentence. In one fell swoop, you are being gracious, but you're also ending the exchange. I mean, what else is there to say after that? Except for, "You're welcome," which, frankly, I don't hear that often. Instead, what I do often hear, just as I'm about to take a bite of my lunch, is "I hate to ask you this, but . . ." and then the stranger who just said this sheepishly holds up her phone and asks if she can have just one picture of me, or a sleeve will be pushed up and I'll be asked to sign an arm, and I oblige, but I'm always . . . always thinking. . . .

If you hate to ask, why are you asking? And I mean that with all due respect.

If I weren't such a people pleaser, then maybe I'd have the balls to say something like this, but I usually say, "Sure," or, "Of course," and on some level I really mean it, because I know that this person—even when they've confused me with someone who used to date Jim Carrey—has shown some interest in me and my work, and I am always grateful for this.

Because we all want to be liked, right? Even when we're being told by someone we don't know from Adam that we—or our work—suck.

IS THERE AN APP FOR THAT?

Sometimes I wish I could wake up in the morning and turn on an app that would be kind of like a preprogrammed personal GPS. That way all I'd have to do would be turn it on so that Siri or whatever her name is would just say, "Turn left here," and then, "Turn right here." And then things like, "Okay, honey. Sit down and take a breather for ten minutes." Maybe she could even make me a sandwich. And rub my shoulders. Maybe even fold the laundry?

Do you ever have this feeling? Do you ever have find yourself, say, in your house and you're walking with determination and then you just come to a full stop and find that you no longer have any idea of where you're going or what you were about to do? This is where I need that Siri person to chime in and say, "You were going to get the toolbox, because you need that tiny screwdriver, because the batteries need to be changed in that little thingie. . . ."

So there's that kind of GPSing I could use.

But there's also a larger, more existential kind of guidance I'd like. I mean, wouldn't it be nice if someone (by someone I mean an electronically soothing voice that had no discernible accent and spoke in a reliably emotionless way) chimed in and said, "You need to take on this project because it's going to be a real game changer for you." Or, "This is not the house you should buy, because the foundation really sucks." Or, "I know he doesn't look like your type, but I'm telling you . . ."

This "Siri" would be like the ultimate life coach, spiritual guru, best friend, and mother all rolled into one: She'd be like my own private Zoltar, the fortune-teller.

I guess I'm riffing on all of this at this particular moment because I'm still working to get my own personal bearings in a way. I mean, sure, there are the girls and all their stuff, and I have no complaints there. But after the dishes are done and the girls are off doing their own thing, sometimes I find my compass kind of goes flat and I'll be overcome with that sense of, "What am I doing here? What is the meaning of it all?" And then I'll get a little anxious because I feel, at least at that moment, that I've got to know what the next steps are and how to plot them on a map and then how to set myself in motion.

Broken compass. Blank map. Not sure which way to turn.

I guess there are two ways of looking at this: I am either everywhere—or nowhere. I am either really living in the present and not worrying about the future, or I'm seriously short a game plan. Depending on what day it is, I can see this from either side. And if I'm feeling all Zen and light, it's kind of cool not knowing what my next steps will be. If I'm feeling a bit insecure or lonely or hungry, it feels like a massive failure on my part, as though my personal transportation department has gone on strike and I'm just stranded, with no clue where I'm supposed to be headed or how to get there. But then I think (better brace yourself: This is extremely deep), do any of us really know where we're going? Or, more to the point, aren't we all going to wind up at the same final destination, no matter which route we take to get there?

When I get all philosophical like this, I realize it's not a bad way to be. I mean, people who act like they've got it all figured out? Well, this is me calling bullshit.

Those people don't have better information than I have; they're just more confident about the bits and pieces of information that they do have.

In the end, that's where I could use a bit more help. I just wish I felt a bit more confident in my own GPS, wish I felt like I could pretty much count on everything being A-OK around that next corner.

That's why I think it's high time someone made that app, the algorithm that crunches your deepest-longing data and gives you the road map for your one true, perfect life.

I've actually given this concept so much thought that I've tried to make this work, using Google Maps. I've done things like type in the word *enlightenment*, and a place quite near me in LA actually popped up. Well, it was a business called something like Enlightenment and Compassionate Healing or something, and I read the review, and I'm pretty sure it's a weed shop. But this emboldened me, so next I typed in *heaven's gate*, and this turned out to be a mere 10,360 miles from my current location, in South Africa somewhere. That would entail way too many travel arrangements, so that's out. Next I typed in *peaceful valley*, and that's a reasonable 825 miles northeast, in Colorado. All I'd really have to do is gas up the ol' Rover and . . . I'm there.

But you know what? Maybe I don't need a GPS at all. I mean, when I first landed in LA, I got around, got jobs, got a life, all using the big, clunky Yellow Pages and blue *Thomas Guide*. And before that, I did just fine without even so much as a cell phone. Maybe I don't need someone else to invent that app after all. Maybe I'll find my way all on my own, the old-fashioned way.

THREE LITTLE BIRDIES

Growing up I always had this weird sixth sense that one day I was going to give birth to three boys. I don't know why, and at least I got the three part right. Whether it's girls or boys, once you become a parent, you are forever transformed. We are all, mothers and fathers, hardwired to care for our little cherubs, and I feel certain that, were I ever put in the terrible predicament of risking my life in order to save one of my girls, I would do it without question.

I think that's the big gift of parenthood: It takes your focus off of yourself and turns it outward, so that it rests on others. Your selfishness becomes something else, something . . . selfless. There are degrees of selflessness, of course. You've all heard the instruction that is repeated, whenever you are buckling up on an airplane, to "put the oxygen mask on yourself first." This reminder is particularly important for those traveling with small children, because were the shit to hit the fan thirty-five thousand feet up, most of us would dive for the wee ones, then keel over for lack of oxygen before we could be much help to them. So it's helpful to be reminded to take care of yourself first, especially if, like me, you tend to be a people pleaser and to neglect yourself—and your needs—by busying yourself with the needs of your kids.

No one, of course, asks us to do this. But then again, no one is encouraging most young women who are single and working and doing what they can to be a sound family of one to take good care of themselves either.

I think it's all about finding that balance point: the fulcrum where you can sit and see it all, while being pretty still and undisturbed.

I know it's taken me raising not one, not two, but three kids—all girls—to even begin to realize that I've been doing a pretty lousy job of putting that oxygen mask on myself first.

But, hey: It's never too late, right?

This past summer I watched my eldest, who is in high school, head across the country to attend a summer program at a university three thousand miles from us. In New York City. On her own. Watching her leap out into the world with such a strong sense of who she is and such a strong sense of safety and security, I know her dad and I have really done something right. Not to mention the rest of the wise and loving village of friends and family around her, around us, that has helped us raise her well.

You've got to be strong to be a woman these days, and all of my girls have moxie in spades. My littlest, who is all of seven, bowls me over with her awesome fierceness. She is all girl, and she will not be taking any shit. From anyone. Including her mom and dad. But she's the opposite of a brat: She's just got lots and lots of self-respect. I like that in a girl. I love it in my girls. And I love it in myself.

All three of my little birds work hard, play hard, and love well. They aren't afraid to make mistakes, to roll up their sleeves and get dirty, to lose the game, to be cut from the team. They're also not shy about sharing their feelings or their opinions. They are amazing.

I have no idea why, but for some reason, when I was very young, I latched onto the notion that I was meant to be treated like a princess, and that getting up onto the pedestal—and staying there—was the ultimate goal. Where on earth did I pick up this twisted message? Maybe I equated being the baby of a big, blended family—where I always got my way, was always fawned over—maybe I mistook all that doting to mean I was somehow special. Or maybe I was raised in a time when too many Disney fantasy messages were subliminally seeping into my very porous brain. In the end, it doesn't matter where I picked up the "princess" attitude: I held on to it for too long, and in truth, it just messed me up for a lot of years.

I wish I had been knocked off my pedestal earlier in life, before I'd done so much damage—the kind of damage one inflicts on others when one has lost her grounding and convinces herself that she's above it all. I'm not suggesting you need to go knock your kids off their pedestals, literally. I just know—belatedly, it seems—that overromanticizing things negates them. Always looking for the fantasy means you miss out on what is really in front of you. When your head is always in the clouds, in terms of what you believe you deserve, you are bound to experience heartache and disappointment, rather than joy and love.

There is a way to be realistic and loving and kind and lovable all at the same time, and I've spent the better part of my adulthood scrambling around trying to find the person who can show me the way to this more mature way of being. But guess what. Here's where the whole selfless thing just gets turned inside out: The only way you'll find that kind of deep, peaceful contentment is to look within. To turn to yourself. Once you get acquainted with yourself and get real and honest with yourself, only then can you even think about becoming selfless.

For the past couple of years, I've really gotten this, and so I've begun to pour all the energy and resources I used to spend on gurus and shrinks and elixirs and retreats into studying, thoughtfully and gratefully, human relationships. I want to know everything about them: how they work and why they work. I can see now that being in a healthy relationship takes two capable and willing people, each of whom is really good at living his or her own life—so good, in fact, that each is primed and ready to share that life with another. In this kind of loving, intimate exchange, there is *just no room for a princess*. Ironic, isn't it, that I began doing this work at the time when I was no longer in a relationship for the first time in my adult life. But of course! I'm still settling that oxygen mask onto my nose and learning not to fret about whether or not it's messing up my hair.

More than anything, I want to be a good role model for my girls, or at least a realistic one. I want them to see that I'm strong enough to make mistakes and wise enough to learn from them. That I may be old in their eyes, but that I haven't stopped growing up. They have seen me fall for sure; they've been right there, front and center, when I crumpled and cried. Sometimes I cringe when I realize that they've seen the real me—the person with all the messy, complicated feelings—and not the polished blonde with the impeccable makeup and the flawless, handsomely-paid-for style. Sure, they've gotten the red-carpet me, but even better, they've gotten the real me, the one who struggles and falls and fails, and I do not regret that.

And I want my girls to feel things—I mean, really *feel* them. I don't want them to just skate through life—I want them to be fully engaged. Fully present. Fully alive.

I will know I've loved really well and that I've become a successful person when I get to see my three little birdies spread their wings and fly.

DEEP THOUGHTS

Now you know it's true: We blondes really do have deep thoughts. I mean, just today I thought: *I wonder why Ray's Pizza stopped using canned mushrooms and started using fresh? Dang it, I hate fresh mushrooms.*

Since I'm into being honest these days, I will say I have spent a fair amount of my blonde life doing everything possible to avoid having to think or, more frankly, feel things on too deep a level. I don't know if it was just a control thing or a princess thing or a sorry combination of both, but when it came down to juggling the hard feelings we're all handed, well . . . let's just say I dropped more than my fair share of balls in my day.

But lately, that's begun to change.

For Christmas last year my fifteen-year-old gave me a lovely little hardcover book entitled *Shit Happens So Get Over It*. At the time I was still so raw and sad and steeped in self-pity that I took her gesture the wrong way. I felt like she wanted to hurt me, to tell me to "stop being sad Mom already." I didn't know how to react, so I just laughed, said thanks, then hid the book away.

Enough time has passed now, however, and I'm ready to receive the message. I was just too invested in my story, too busy gnawing on my own wounds when Luca gave that book to me to see the bigger picture. Well, of course she wasn't being insensitive. On the contrary, she was trying to express the truth that we all go through bad times; we all get hurt; we all grieve. It was a beautiful teenage way of saying, "I see what you're going through. I get it, Mom."

One day, not too long ago, I found that little book and I started to page through it. It's an easy read, even for a blonde. It's full of pearls of wisdom like "Sometimes you just have to pee in the sink" by Charles Bukowski. And "You can't be brave if you've only had wonderful things happen to you" by Mary Tyler Moore. I kept turning the pages and reading and I found myself smiling and chuckling. Finally—I was getting it! It took only six months, but I was finally getting the gist of Luca's gift.

Now I keep Luca's little present prominently displayed on the coffee table in our living room. I'm sure there are people who come to the house who think, "Is this really the best kind of reading material to have around young girls?" My answer to that would be a resounding yes. Yes, it is. So get over it.

Life is going to be hard and bumpy, and it's not going to do what you want it to do when you want it to: It is going to keep going, and you've got to keep going along with it, or else you will miss out. I have been so stubborn, so resistant. I didn't want to get divorced. I didn't want my family to break apart. Well, guess what. It happened. And yet we're all still here—me, the girls, their dad—and we're all still living life. But we can live well and be free and happy only when we accept it. And by *it* I mean accepting all of it: the good, the bad, the disappointing, the heartbreaking. We just have to let life happen.

ACKNOWLEDGMENTS

My deep thanks go to:

Randy and Kelle for "discovering" me and for making me believe in love.

Carolyn Garth for supporting my journey at every turn, and teaching me that there's nothing I can't do.

John Morris Garth for sitting quietly with me in the woods.

My siblings: Cammie, Lisa, Wendy, Lynn, John, and Chuck for keeping me grounded and loving me so much.

Emily for her patience and enthusiasm in helping with this book, and for hearing and understanding my voice.

Adele for waxing my woodle and giving me years of unparalleled free therapy.

Patrice, Jazzy, Jensen, and Derwood for taco nights.

Steve and Andy for not stealing my money.

Nina for loving my babies like they are her own, and Juan for lending us Nina!

Peter for giving me the three most important things in my life, and the biggest gift ever . . .

My team: Liz, Stephanie, Melis, Clarina, Nicole, Jennifer, my agents Jack, Iris, and Irwin, Astrid, Jessica Wu, Cindy, Wade, Sherri, Erin, Jamie and Daniella, my Michael, Bryan, Dana, Andre, Daniel, and Marlene.

Jen Schuster and everyone at Penguin who helped make this book happen.

Tori, Shannen, Jason, Ian, Brian, and Luke.

The El Encanto, a great writing cave.

Any guy brave enough to date me after my divorce.

Cupcakes everywhere.

The Hamer family.

The Picard family.

Emily Heckman's Acknowledgments

Beautiful work with a beautiful team: JG, RJ, JS, LL, I thank you.

This one is for EB, with love.—EH